Miracle Moments
in
NEW YORK YANKEES
History

The Turning Points, the Memorable Games, the Incredible Records

DAVID FISCHER

SPORTS
PUBLISHING

Sports Publishing books may be purchased in bulk at special discounts for sales promotion, corporate gifts, fund-raising, or educational purposes. Special editions can also be created to specifications. For details, contact the Special Sales Department, Sports Publishing, 307 West 36th Street, 11th Floor, New York, NY 10018 or sportspubbooks@skyhorsepublishing.com.

Sports Publishing® is a registered trademark of Skyhorse Publishing, Inc.®, a Delaware corporation.

Visit our website at www.sportspubbooks.com.

10 9 8 7 6 5 4 3 2 1

Library of Congress Cataloging-in-Publication Data is available on file.

Cover design by Tom Lau
Cover photo credit: Associated Press

ISBN: 978-1-61321-998-0
Ebook ISBN: 978-1-68358-002-7

Printed in China

TO THE PLAYERS AND COACHES OF THE 2010
12U NEW JERSEY BANDITS BASEBALL TEAM;
YOUR ACCOMPLISHMENTS WERE A TURNING POINT IN MY LIFE,
AND I THANK YOU FOR ALL THE MEMORABLE GAMES YOU PLAYED AND THE
INCREDIBLE RECORDS YOU SET.
WHOOSH!

Contents

Introduction   ix

Part One:
Birth of a Dynasty   1
1903: From Highlanders to Yankees   3
1904: The First Star   5
1912: Donning Pinstripes   7
1920: Here Comes the Babe   10
1923: The House That Ruth Built   13
1927: Murderers' Row   16
1932: The Called Shot   20
1934: Larrupin' Lou   23

Part Two:
The Bronx Bombers   27

1936: Poosh 'Em Up Tony   29
1937: DiMaggio Breaks Out   32
1939: "The Luckiest Man"   37
1941: Joe DiMaggio's Hitting Streak   44
1941: The Missed Third Strike   40
1943: Dickey Soldiers On   46
1947: One Out From Immortality   49
1949: Yankees Steal a Pennant   51

Part Three:
Mickey, Casey, Whitey, and Yogi   55

1953: Mantle's Tape Measure Homer   57
1953: Five-Peat   59
1955: It's Déjà vu All Over Again   64
1956: The Mick's Triple Crown   68
1956: World Series Perfection   72
1957: Incident at the Copa   75
1960: Mazeroski Slays Goliath   78
1961: 61 in '61   80
1961: Ford Keeps Rolling   83
1962: Terry's Redemption   86
1964: End of the Dynasty   89

Part Four:
The Bronx Zoo   93

1973: The Boss   95
1973: The First Designated Hitter   98

1974: Reeling in a Catfish 101
1976: Chambliss Delivers 103
1977: Mr. October 106
1978: Louisiana Lightning 110
1978: Bullpen Aces 113
1978: Dent's Monster Moment 117
1978: The Comeback Kids 119
1979: A Yankee Tragedy 121
1981: Down Goes Frazier 124
1983: The Pine Tar Game 128
1987: Donnie Baseball 132
1993: Inspiration Personified 135

Part Five:
The Core Four 139

1996: A New Dynasty Emerges 141
1998: Boomer's Big Day 147
1999: Finally Perfect 150
1999: Yankees Sweep Again 153
2000: Subway Series 157
2001: The Flip Play 161
2001: Mystique and Aura 164
2003: Boone Blasts Boston 168
2005: A-Rod's Big Night 171
2008: From Catcher to Manager 175
2008: The Captain Closes the Stadium 180
2009: Godzilla Conquers Gotham 184
2011: Mo Is Money 189
2011: Mr. 3,000 191
2016: Baby Bombers 195

References   **199**

Acknowledgments   **201**

INTRODUCTION

The New York Yankees have won more World Series championships than any other major league club. They are, by far, the most successful franchise in sports history.

The Yankees won their first pennant in 1921. It was their first of twenty-nine pennants and twenty World Series championships in the forty-four seasons between 1921 and 1964. Yankee players recorded some of baseball's most memorable streaks, records and achievements during this era. Babe Ruth hit 60 home runs in 1927, a mark that stood for thirty-four years until 1961 when another Yankee slugger, Roger Maris, swatted 61 long flies. Lou Gehrig had an ironman streak of 2,130 consecutive games played, a record for fifty-six years. And Joe DiMaggio hit in 56 consecutive games in 1941, a record that still stands seventy-five years later.

The Yankees had an abundance of talent starting with Ruth, a player many consider the greatest ever to play the game. His most memorable home run was his "called-shot" in the fifth inning of Game 3 of the 1932 World Series against the Cubs at Wrigley Field. Still unclear is Ruth's intention; did he point to a spot in centerfield where his shot would land or to the Cubs bench to answer their relentless taunting? Ruth played two more seasons after that with New York, but by the early '30s Lou Gehrig was New York's greatest player.

Gehrig is generally regarded as the greatest first baseman in history, and would be so noted even if not for his incredible durability. When Gehrig was finally forced out of the lineup early in 1939 due to an incurable disease, the Yankees declared July 4, 1939, as Lou Gehrig Day, and honored him between games of a double-header. His moving speech will never be forgotten.

Another major turning point for the Yankees franchise was the arrival of Joe DiMaggio onto the team in 1936. He was one of the top three players of his generation—and one of the best and most graceful outfielders of all time. The Yankees won the World Series in each of his first four seasons. Years later, when DiMaggio's career began to decline due to age and a series of heel injuries, a young center fielder named Mickey Mantle was ready to assume his place in the dynasty. Mantle was the best switch-hitter of all time, and possessed the rare combination of power and speed.

But the Yankees didn't just feature great sluggers. Pitcher Whitey Ford anchored the staff throughout the 1950s and early '60s. And a journeyman, Don Larsen, would pitch a perfect game in Game 5 of the 1956 World Series. Other perfect games and no-hitters would follow, but no Yankees pitcher enjoyed as dominant a season as Ron Guidry did in 1978.

Following a tough seven-game loss to the Cardinals in the 1964 World Series, the franchise slid into the second division and languished there for nearly a decade. But in 1973, a Cleveland shipbuilder named George Steinbrenner bought the team from CBS for less than $10 million. The Yankees went on to win pennants in 1976, 1977, and 1978, winning the World Series in both '77 and '78. After losing the 1976 World Series, Steinbrenner signed free-agent slugger Reggie Jackson. Jackson added a turbulent mix to the clubhouse, but the move paid off when he hit three home runs in Game 6 of the 1977 World Series. The Yankees came from 14 games behind Boston to catch the Red Sox in 1978. The Yankees lost their captain—catcher Thurman Munson—to a plane crash in August of 1979. After winning 103 games and losing in the A.L.C.S. in 1980, the Yankees went to the World Series once again in 1981.

The Yankees didn't return to the postseason until 1995, but only because the 70-43 Yankee team in 1994 had their season suspended by the player lockout. The Yankees made the postseason in 1995, the first of 13 consecutive postseason appearances. New York won the World Series in 1996, 1998, 1999, 2000, and 2009. These teams were led by relief ace Mariano Rivera, perhaps the greatest closer in baseball history; and by shortstop Derek Jeter, one of the biggest stars of his generation.

Throughout its illustrious history, the New York Yankees have produced some of the most memorable highlights in baseball annals. Jack Chesbro's 41 wins in a season, Tony Lazzeri's 11 RBIs in a game, Derek Jeter's amazing "Flip Play," and Aaron Boone's walk-off homer to propel the Yankees into another World Series. Most Yankees fans have seen newsreel footage of Yogi Berra's unorthodox swing, and watched highlights of a young Don Mattingly, and have heard the story of Phil Linz's harmonica playing. But what makes the Yankees the world's most celebrated sports franchise goes beyond sheer headlines: it is the stories of the men behind the headlines who have thrilled and enchanted New York fans since 1903.

PART ONE

BIRTH OF A DYNASTY

Batting practice at Hilltop Park, 1911 (George Grantham Bain Collection, Library of Congress)

1903

From Highlanders to Yankees

The New York Yankees were born in 1903, but under a different name.. The team was transplanted from Baltimore to give the upstart American League a team in New York to compete with the more established National League's New York Giants. The original home of the Yankees was Hilltop Park, a small, hastily built, wooden ballpark with a grandstand to seat 15,000 fans and a centerfield fence 560 feet away from home plate. The park was located in Manhattan along upper Broadway between 165th and 168th Streets, at one of the highest spots in New York City.

This new American League team still needed a name. At first, the team was going to be called the Americans, but then most people called them the Highlanders because of their home ballpark's high elevation. Newspapers introduced the nickname "Yankees" to reference the club's location—to the north of the Giants. A majority of sportswriters at the time were loyal to the Giants and viewed the new competition as the enemy. By 1904 "Yankees" was already popular in the papers and commonly abbreviated as Yanks, but the name was not yet official.

The Highlanders lost the first game they ever played, 3-1, to the Senators in Washington, D.C., on April 22, 1903. The next day, with Harry Howell on the hill, the Highlanders beat the Senators, 7-2, to capture the first win in franchise history. Seven days later, back in New York, the Highlanders beat the Senators 6-2 to record a win in their home opener at Hilltop Park. More history occurred when John Ganzel hit the franchise's first home run, in the fifth inning of a game against the Tigers, on May 11, 1903. It was an inside-the-park home run off George Mullin at Bennett Park in Detroit.

John Ganzel hit the first home run for the New York franchise in
1903. (George Grantham Bain Collection, Library of Congress)

The team finished its inaugural season in fourth place; it would take another 20 years
for the first World Series title. The Highlanders played in Hilltop Park until 1912. When
the team's lease on Hilltop Park ran out, they worked out a deal with the Giants to sub-
let the Polo Grounds. Prior to moving into the Polo Grounds for the 1913 season, the
Highlanders officially changed their name to the Yankees. That proved to be a wise choice.

1904

The First Star

Jack Chesbro pitched the very first game in the history of the New York Yankees, then known as the Highlanders, on April 22, 1903. The Yankees lost the game, 3-1, in Washington, D.C. that day, but did very little losing when Chesbro pitched thereafter. By the end of the following season, Chesbro was the winningest pitcher in the game. Using his masterful spitball to great effect, Chesbro threw a four-hit, complete game to beat the Boston Red Sox (then known as the Pilgrims), 3-2, on October 7, 1904. It was a respectable effort for the 30-year-old right-hander; what made it extraordinary was that it was Chesbro's 41st win of the season, a modern major league record that still stands.

Chesbro produced eye-popping pitching statistics in 1904, but is best remembered for his final pitch of that ill-fated season. The Yankees were in a neck-and-neck battle with the Red Sox. On October 10, the last day of the season, the teams met in a doubleheader at Hilltop Park in New York. Boston was in first place, one game ahead of the New Yorkers. To win the pennant, the Yankees needed to win both games of the doubleheader. With Chesbro on the mound for the first game, their chances looked promising.

But Chesbro had his hands full, dueling Boston's Bill Dinneen through eight innings. When Chesbro strode from the dugout to start the top of the ninth inning, the score was tied at 2-2. Boston catcher Lou Criger opened with a single. A sacrifice bunt put him on second base. An infield out moved him to third. Chesbro needed only one out to get out of the inning. The 30,000 New York fans were confident that Chesbro would work out of the jam when the count on the batter reached one ball and two strikes. Then Chesbro uncorked a spitball that sailed over the catcher's head to the backstop, allowing the go-ahead run to score. When New York failed to score in the bottom of the ninth, the pennant was clinched for Boston. The Highlanders had lost on Chesbro's wild pitch. For years, fans said it was the costliest wild pitcher ever thrown by a pitcher.

Chesbro had been enjoying a dream season in 1904. He won 41 games, six by shut-out, lost only 12, with a miniscule 1.82 earned run average. He completed 48 of 51 starts—including his first 30 starts in a row—and pitched four games in relief. He pitched 454.2 innings, and allowed just 338 hits. During a particularly dominant stretch he won 14 consecutive games, and pitched 40 straight scoreless innings. He would lead the American League in wins, winning percentage, games started, complete games, and innings pitched. It had been a magical season for Chesbro—until the wild pitch.

"Happy" Jack Chesbro won 19 games in 1905 and 23 in 1906, before retiring in 1909 with 198 career victories. He was forever haunted by the wild pitch until his death in 1931. Friends are said to have lobbied the commissioner's office to change the official scorer's decision to a passed ball, but without success. Chesbro was elected to the Hall of Fame in 1946. His plaque incorrectly credits him with only 192 victories. It says nothing about the wild pitch.

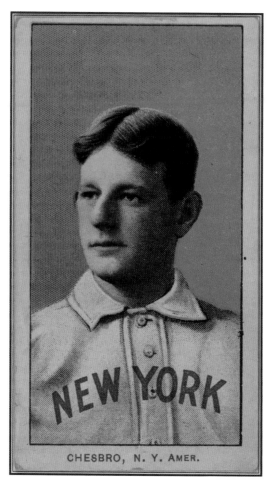

CHESBRO, N. Y. AMER.

Jack Chesbro. (From the Benjamin K. Edwards Collection, Library of Congress)

1912

Donning Pinstripes

The Yankees' interlocking NY monogram is the most recognizable insignia in all of sports. The insignia was inspired by a design created by renowned jeweler Louis C. Tiffany in 1877 for a medal to honor a New York City policeman shot in the line of duty. Bill Devery, one of the club's early owners and a former New York City police chief, liked the design so much he adopted it for the organization. Today, the Yankees' cap with its interlocking NY is worn as a fashion statement not only to express one's fandom, but also as a valentine for New York City.

The Yankees' uniform evolved from several iterations during the early days. When the Yankees, then called the Highlanders, began play in 1903, their uniform jersey sported a large N on the right breast and a large Y on the left breast. In 1905, the N and Y were merged on the left breast, creating a prototype of the now legendary emblem. Four years later, the monogram made its first appearance on the players' cap and left sleeve of the Highlanders' jersey.

In their final season at Hilltop Park the Highlanders made a fashion statement for the 1912 home opener by taking the field wearing pinstripes for the first time in franchise history. Pinstripes were a popular look at the time, as eight of the 15 major league teams wore striped uniforms. The Highlanders abandoned the pinstripes during their first two seasons sharing the Polo Grounds with the New York Giants, but by 1915, the pinstripes on the home uniform were back for good.

The Yankees removed the NY monogram from the jersey in 1917—though the NY remained on the cap—and for the next two decades the team favored the pinstripes-only look. It wasn't until 1936 that the interlocking NY was restored to the Yankees uniform, meaning that Babe Ruth, who played for the Yankees from 1920 to 1934, played his entire Yankees career without ever sporting the club's legendary insignia on his jersey. The Yankees home uniform has remained mostly unchanged for more than eighty years.

New York Yankees president Frank Farrell presents a loving cup to Yankees manager Harry Wolverton as Red Sox and Yankees players look on at Hilltop Park, New York, April 11, 1912. Wolverton sports an early version of the Yankees logo on his jersey. (George Grantham Bain Collection, Library of Congress)

The Yankees wore different style caps from 1903 to 1921, including a white cap with pinstripes in 1921, before finally settling on the team's signature look, a solid navy cap with interlocking NY insignia in 1922.

The club's road uniforms—solid gray with NEW YORK in block letters across the chest—have remained relatively unchanged since 1918. Teams wore dark uniforms for road games to help fans tell the visiting team from the home team. This tradition began around 1890. Back then, baseball teams chose to wear gray during road games for another reason, too: They rarely had places to wash their uniforms on road trips. The gray color hid dirt and stains—sort of. Fans still complained that visiting teams looked grubby, and players complained about the aroma in the visitors' dugout.

In 1929, the defending world champion New York Yankees and the Cleveland Indians became the first teams to wear permanent numbers sewn onto the backs of their uniform jerseys. Starting players were given numbers that matched their usual place in the batting order. That's why Babe Ruth wore number 3; because he usually batted third.

The numbers and corresponding names were listed in the club's scorecards, and so, perhaps, also marked the first time ballpark vendors called out: "Scorecards, get your scorecards, here. You can't tell the players without a scorecard."

Other major league teams quickly adopted the idea and, by the late 1930s, uniform numbers became standard for all teams.

Unconventional team owner Bill Veeck introduced player names to the back of his Chicago White Sox jerseys in spring training of 1960. The idea was an immediate success, brought about by the popularity of baseball on television, and today, every big league team has adopted the practice with one notable exception. Despite being the first major league club to adopt permanent uniform numbers, the tradition-minded New York Yankees have yet to don a uniform (home or road) adorned with player names.

1920

Here Comes the Babe

The decade known as the Roaring Twenties jumped out of the starting gate when, on January 3, 1920, the Boston Red Sox sold the best baseball player of all time, Babe Ruth, to the New York Yankees. No question, this was the greatest signing in sports history.

Consider the fortunes of both franchises at the time. In 1920, the Yankees were then a seventeen-year-old team that had never won a pennant. The Red Sox were World Series winners four times over the past eight years. Babe Ruth, only twenty-four, had already led the American League in home runs two seasons in a row. But the Babe made trouble off the field for Red Sox owner Harry Frazee, who was also a theatrical producer. According to legend, Frazee was riddled with debt and desperately needed money to finance his new Broadway show, *No! No! Nanette*. But Frazee simply had grown frustrated with Ruth's constant demands for a raise in salary. In a deal that has haunted Boston baseball fans ever since, Frazee sold Ruth to New York for over $100,000 and a $385,000 loan.

The Yankees immediately doubled Ruth's salary—at his demand—to a then unheard of $20,000 a year. No athlete had ever been paid so much. But the Babe was worth every penny. In his first season with the Yankees, Ruth hit 54 home runs. By July 19 he had already broken his own record of 29 homers, set the year before. No other American league *team* hit as many homers as Ruth did in 1920. He was primarily responsible for the Yankees becoming the first club to draw more than 1 million fans in a single season.

Ruthian became a word to describe the Babe's extraordinary feats. Once seen, the Ruthian homer was

Harry Frazee, the man who traded Babe Ruth to the Yankees. (George Grantham Bain Collection, Library of Congress)

never forgotten. Most home run hitters power the ball into the seats or over the wall on either a line or a high arc. But Ruth's hits soared lazily skyward to dizzying heights, then carried farther and farther from the plate. When they dropped, they seemed to drop straight down. Even the shots that stayed in the park often amazed fans.

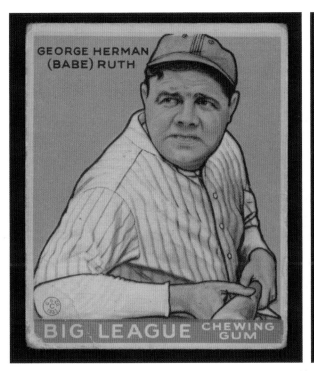
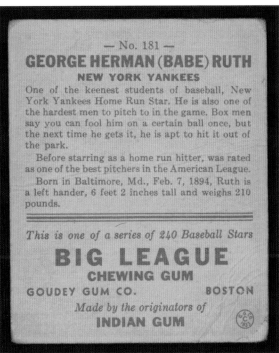

Babe Ruth's baseball card, front and back, circa 1933. (Goudey Gum Co., Library of Congress)

"No one hit home runs the way Babe did," said Dizzy Dean, a Hall of Fame pitcher for the Cardinals. "They were something special, like homing pigeons. The ball would leave the bat, pause briefly, suddenly gain its bearings, then take off for the stands."

The only thing Ruth failed to do in his first spectacular season in New York was lead the Yankees to the pennant. Still, the sale of Ruth became the single most important—and infamous—deal in sports history. It dramatically reversed the World Series fortunes of both teams. The Yankees would win twenty-six World Series by the end of the century, becoming the most successful team in professional sports. The Red Sox didn't even play in another World Series until 1946, and the team would not win a World Series for eighty-six years, often failing in heartbreaking fashion. Many fans believed it was Ruth's curse upon them.

CURSE OF THE BAMBINO

The phrase "Curse of the Bambino" became popular following a 1990 book by the same title by *Boston Globe* sports columnist Dan Shaughnessy. The book chronicles the classic BoSox debacles, from Johnny Pesky's holding the ball in the seventh game of the 1946 World Series, to Bucky Dent's deflating home run in the deciding game of the 1978 season, to the horrifying dribbler that slithered

Babe Ruth in 1919. (National Photo Company Collection, Library of Congress)

between Bill Buckner's legs one out away from a Series victory in 1986, to Aaron Boone's stunning extra-inning home run in the final game of the 2003 playoffs.

Mining such heartbreak led the author Stephen King to give one of publishing's all-time great book-jacket blurbs: "The quintessential New England horror story. Read it and weep."

Then in 2004 the world changed. Boston and New York met again in the ALCS, with Boston becoming the first team in major league history to come back to win a playoff series after being down three games to none. Then Boston defeated St. Louis in the World Series to win their first championship since 1918 and thus end the Curse of the Bambino.

1923

The House That Ruth Built

The arrival of Babe Ruth in New York City caused the turnstiles to spin like never before at the Polo Grounds, which the Yankees had shared with the New York Giants since 1913. Spurred on by his fantastic long balls, fans flocked to ballparks to watch the Babe in action. In 1920, Ruth's first season with the Yankees, they became the first major league team to draw more than one million fans (officially 1,289,422) in a single season.

As landlord, the New York Giants were not happy playing second fiddle to the guests, and notified the Yankees to vacate the premises as soon as possible. When the Giants told the Yankees to leave the Polo Grounds, Colonel Jacob Ruppert, co-owner of the New York Yankees, declared, "I want the greatest ballpark in the world." He got his wish.

In February 1921, the Yankees purchased ten acres of property from the estate of William Waldorf Astor at 161st Street and River Avenue in the west Bronx, directly across the Harlem River from the Polo Grounds. The Yankees owners Ruppert and Tillinghast Huston announced the construction of baseball's first triple-decked structure. With a capacity of over 70,000, it would also be the first structure to be called a "stadium."

The Osborn Engineering Company of Cleveland designed the park. It was the first stadium to have three decks, the first to ring its grandstand with the 16-foot copper façade that became its trademark, the first to house as many as 60,000 seats, and the first to have a flagpole and monuments in the field of play.

The White Construction Company of New York broke ground on the site on May 5, 1922. Incredibly, the stadium was built in only 284 working days and at a price of $2.5 million. The framework eventually involved 2,200 tons of structural steel and more than one million brass screws. Materials used to form the playing field included 13,000 cubic yards of earth, topped by 116,000 square feet of sod.

The new Yankee Stadium would favor left-handed power hitters with a right-field foul pole only 295 feet from home plate. Because it was widely recognized that Ruth's tremendous drawing power had made the new stadium possible, Fred Lieb of the *Evening Telegram* called the stadium "the House That Ruth Built," and the name stuck.

Yankee Stadium opened on April 18, 1923, with all the pomp and circumstance fitting the new king of baseball stadiums. According to the *New York Times*, 74,217 fans packed themselves inside, and thousands more were turned away by the fire department "convinced that baseball parks are not nearly as large as they should be."

Babe Ruth and teammates during the pregame ceremony at the opening of Yankee Stadium in 1923. (George Grantham Bain Collection, Library of Congress)

In pregame festivities, John Phillip Sousa and the Seventh Regiment Band raised the *Stars and Stripes* and the Yankees' 1922 pennant at the flagpole in deep center field. New York's governor, Al Smith, threw out the first ball. Ruth told a reporter, "I'd give a year of my life to hit a home run today."

Fittingly, he did. Ruth, always able to rise to the occasion, christened the new ballpark in the Bronx by slamming the first home run in Yankee Stadium history—a three-run shot off Howard Ehmke to help Bob Shawkey and the Yankees capture a 4-1 victory over the Red Sox, Ruth's former team.

The Yankees, led by manager Miller Huggins, opened the new stadium to great fanfare by reaching the World Series. The Yankees reached the World Series in 1921 and 1922, each time facing the rival New York Giants in a Polo Grounds World Series. Since the Yankees were then playing their home games in the Giants' ballpark, the teams exchanged dugouts between games. The Giants won the series both years.

In 1923, each team again won their respective pennants, setting up a Yankees-Giants World Series for a third straight season. But this match-up had a plot twist. The 1923 World Series was the first Subway Series. The subway had become the main form of public transportation in the city and was a convenient way to travel between ballparks. The Yankees, in their first year in the new Yankee Stadium, gained a measure of revenge by clinching their first-ever championship in a Game 6 win on the very Polo Grounds field from which they'd been evicted. Ruth batted .368, walked eight times, scored eight runs, and walloped three home runs to help the team to the first of their twenty-seven world championships. Said owner Ruppert: "Now I have the greatest ballpark and the greatest team."

1927

Murderers' Row

It's easy to start an argument among baseball fans. All you need do, for example, is tell a Yankees follower that Leo Durocher was a far better manager than Casey Stengel. Or that Willie Mays could have run rings around Mickey Mantle. You can get some mighty sharp retorts, too, when trying to name the greatest ball team of all time—although you would be hard-pressed to top the New York Yankees of 1927. For this was a team that had everything—speed, crushing power, and a marvelous defense.

Lou Gehrig, Babe Ruth, Earle Combs, and Tony Lazzeri at Fenway Park, 1927. (Courtesy of the Boston Public Library, Leslie Jones Collection)

A stereoscope of Lou Gehrig taken in 1930. (Keystone View Company, Library of Congress)

The 1927 Yankees started the season in first place—and finished in first place. The winning margin? Nineteen games. The number of victories? One hundred ten, at that time an American League record. To climax their historic season, the Yankees swept the Pittsburgh Pirates, 4-0, in the World Series. As Casey would say: "You could look it up."

Certainly, teams have won more regular-season games. The 1906 Chicago Cubs and the 2001 Seattle Mariners both won 116. Neither of those teams won the World Series, though. The 1998 Yankees won 114 games and, like their pinstriped predecessors, swept the Series. Still, there was something so dominant about the 1927 Yankees that even now it is just about impossible to rank any other team above them.

Start with Babe Ruth, who, batting third in the lineup, broke his own home run record by one, blasting 60 homers—the first man to reach that total (his record stood until Roger Maris hit 61 in 1961). Batting fourth was Lou Gehrig, who hit 47 home runs, the most any player not named Ruth had ever whacked in one season. Gehrig also had a record-setting 173 runs batted in. Who knows how many more RBI Gehrig might have had if Ruth hadn't homered so often right before him in the lineup? Then again, Gehrig helped prevent Ruth from achieving the Triple Crown, since he was the only player in the American League who had more RBI (Ruth had 164) and he also had a higher batting average than the Babe.

But Ruth and Gehrig didn't do all the hitting for the Yankees. Four players drove in more than 100 runs. The team batting average was .307 and didn't have a regular player bat under .269. Gehrig batted .373. Ruth and center fielder Earle Combs hit .356 and Combs led the league in singles. Second baseman Tony Lazzeri batted .309 and pounded out 18 homers, the third-best in the league behind Ruth and Gehrig. All four would

Waite Hoyt won 22 games for the Yankees in 1927. (George Grantham Bain Collection, Library of Congress)

one day enter the Baseball Hall of Fame. So fearsome was the hitting of this group that it became known as "Murderer's Row." Only one pitcher, the legendary Lefty Grove of the Philadelphia Athletics, was able to hold the Yankees scoreless in 1927. In a tingling ball game, the A's won 1-0.

Baseball teams do not win pennants without good pitching. The Yankees of 1927 certainly had their share of it, with four pitchers winning 18 or more games. Waite Hoyt won 22 games, and Herb Pennock won another 19. Much of the credit for the performance of the mound staff, however, went to a relief pitcher—Wilcy "Cy" Moore. This "fireman" appeared in 50 games and won 19 times. Urban Shocker added 18 victories.

The numbers are mind-numbing, but how better to display this team's outrageous power? Legend has it that the Pirates were so intimidated watching the Yankees take batting practice before the first game of the World Series that actually playing the games was merely a formality. Indeed, it's hard to believe there was ever a better baseball team than the Yankees of 1927.

YANKEES 100-WIN SEASONS

The Yankees have won 100 or more games in a season 19 times during their history. They won 114 games in 1998 to capture the division title by 22 games over the next closest opponent, their largest margin ever in the standings. In 1927, they won 110 games for a franchise-best .714 winning pace.

The Yankees won 109 games in 1961, 107 games in 1932, and 106 games in 1939, winning a World Series championship in each of those seasons. They won 104 games in 1963 but lost in the Series to the Dodgers.

Year	Won	Lost	Pct.	Place	GA/GB	Manager
1998	114	48	.704	First	+22	Joe Torre
1927	110	44	.714	First	+19	Miller Huggins
1961	109	53	.673	First	+8	Casey Stengel
1932	107	47	.695	First	+13	Joe McCarthy
1939	106	45	.702	First	+17	Joe McCarthy
1963	104	57	.646	First	+10.5	Ralph Houk
1942	103	51	.669	First	+9	Joe McCarthy
1954	103	51	.669	Second	−8	Casey Stengel
1980	103	59	.636	First	+3	Dick Howser
2002	103	58	.640	First	+10.5	Joe Torre
2009	103	59	.636	First	+8	Joe Girardi
1936	102	51	.667	First	+19.5	Joe McCarthy
1937	102	52	.662	First	+13	Joe McCarthy
1928	101	53	.656	First	+2.5	Miller Huggins
1941	101	53	.656	First	+17	Joe McCarthy
2003	101	61	.623	First	+6	Joe Torre
2004	101	61	.623	First	+3	Joe Torre
1977	100	62	.617	First	+2.5	Billy Martin
1978	100	63	.613	First	+1	Martin-Bob Lemon

1932

The Called Shot

The 1932 World Series was Babe Ruth's seventh Series appearance in twelve years with the Yankees. He was at his best in these October showdowns, and his most famous home run of all came in this Series against the Chicago Cubs, at Wrigley Field in Chicago. Ruth took one look at the park's cozy dimensions and salivated. "I'd play for half my salary if I could hit in this dump all the time," he said.

The Yankees were playing the Cubs in game three of the World Series. Charlie Root was pitching for the Cubs and the score was tied, 4-4. Ruth had already hit a three-run homer in the first inning, much to the pleasure of New York governor and Democratic presidential nominee Franklin D. Roosevelt, who was at the game.

When Ruth approached the plate in the top half of the fifth inning, the 49,986 Wrigley Field fans, who had heckled him lustily all day, now yelled insults about his age and weight. Some fans started throwing vegetables at him, while others tossed lemons. According to folklore, the Cubs bench was also directing taunts at the Babe in the form of racial slurs.

What followed depends on whose version of the tale you believe. Root threw strike one, which the fans cheered. Ruth supposedly held up one finger and, according to Cubs catcher Gabby Hartnett, said, "It only takes one to hit it." Root followed by throwing a pair of balls, and then a called strike. The count stood at 2-2. Wrigley Field was ready to explode if Ruth struck out.

Ruth stepped out of the batter's box. Raising his right arm, the Babe pointed. Did Ruth "call" his home run—did he really predict that he would hit it? No one knows for sure. He may have been pointing to the pitcher, or showing the crowd that he still had one more strike. Another possibility is that he might have been gesturing at the Cubs bench, which was filled with players who were teasing him. Or, as legend has it, was he pointing to beyond the outfield fence to indicate where he would hit Root's next pitch?

With the crowd on the edge of their seats, the big-swinging lefty launched that next pitch straight over the centerfield fence to that exact spot, a towering hit that measured 435 feet. It was the longest home run ever hit at Wrigley Field. It was also Ruth's fifteenth, and last, World Series home run. But did Babe really call his shot? No one can be sure. Here are some eyewitness accounts:

"Ruth did point, for sure. He definitely raised his right arm. He indicated [where he'd already] hit a home run. But as far as pointing to center . . . no, he didn't," said Mark Koenig, the Cubs shortstop and Ruth's former Yankee teammate.

Pitcher Charlie Root firmly denied Ruth had pointed at the fence before he swung. Root said: "If he had made a gesture like that, well, anybody who knows me knows that Ruth would have ended up on his [backside]." In 1948, when asked to play himself and re-create the scene for the film biography *The Babe Ruth Story*, Root flatly refused.

Lou Gehrig, who was in the on-deck circle and followed with another homer on the next pitch, said, "Did you see what that big monkey did? He said he'd hit a homer, and he did."

The one man who could definitely answer the question was not saying. "Why don't you read the papers?" Ruth liked to say while flashing a sly smile whenever he was asked if he had called the home run. "It's all right there in the papers."

The Babe never said he did and he never said he didn't. But it doesn't really matter whether or not he actually called that home run. Whatever the facts may be, it is absolutely certain that Ruth always had a flair for the dramatic, and it was heroic enough that in the face of abusive taunts from a large, hostile crowd he came through in the clutch and delivered the punishing, crushing blow that defeated them. The battle over what truly happened in that one moment of time so long ago may never be settled. Still, Babe's "Called Shot" remains one of the most legendary home runs in World Series history. The Yankees went on to sweep the Cubs, the third straight time they won a series without losing a game.

HOME RUN PROMISE

Babe Ruth's called shot in the 1932 World Series was not the first Series home run he dared promise to hit. In 1926, the Yankees had won the pennant by three games over the Cleveland Indians. Ruth was a major factor in that winning season. He belted 47 home runs with 153 RBIs and a .372 batting average. Though the Yankees lost the World Series in seven games to the St. Louis Cardinals, Babe's mark on the series was indelible.

Prior to Game 4, Babe went to a hospital to visit Johnny Sylvester, an eleven-year-old boy who had survived a horse riding accident. To make Johnny feel better, the Babe promised to hit a home run for him in the next game. That game was the first series game ever broadcast on national radio.

Ruth hit one home run, then another, and then a third, becoming the first man to hit three home runs in a single World Series game. The record-breaking third homer was also the first ball ever hit into the centerfield bleachers at Sportsman's Park in St. Louis. When the ball finally came down, an excited radio announcer Graham McNamee called, "What a home run! That is a mile and a half from here." An impressionable Johnny Sylvester would make a full recovery from his injuries.

1934

Larrupin' Lou

Lou Gehrig was born in New York City in 1903, and never strayed too far from his roots. He attended Columbia University and signed with the Yankees in 1923. After a handful of games on the major league level in 1923 and 1924, Gehrig became the Yankees' starting first baseman in 1926, and from then until 1932, he and Babe Ruth were the two greatest hitters ever to play together. Ruth and Gehrig finished first and second, respectively, in the home-run race each season from 1927 to 1931. They scared opposing pitchers in a way two batters had never done before.

Lou Gehrig charges in from first base toward the plate at Fenway Park, 1937. (Courtesy of the Boston Public Library, Leslie Jones Collection)

Gehrig had good seasons in 1925 and 1926, but it was in 1927 as part of the famous "Murderers' Row" Yankees lineup that Gehrig exploded as a superstar. He batted .373 with 47 homers and 175 runs batted in. In spite of Babe Ruth's record 60 home runs in 1927, Lou Gehrig was picked as the American League's most valuable player that year. The 1927 Yankees—considered by many to be the greatest team of all time—swept the Pittsburgh Pirates in the World Series that year.

For the rest of his career Gehrig was the picture of consistency and offensive production. He drove in at least 100 runs for 13 consecutive seasons, topping 150 RBI seven times and setting the American League record with 184 RBI in 1931. He had at least 100 RBI and 100 runs scored in every full season of his career. Oh yeah, and he never missed a game from June 1, 1925 until April 30, 1939, an iron man streak of 2,130 consecutive games played. How's that for consistency?

After sweeping another World Series in 1928, this time from St. Louis, the Yankees took a back seat to Connie Mack's Philadelphia Athletics for three years. On June 3, 1932, Gehrig became the first player in the 20th century to hit four home runs in one game during a 20-13 victory over the A's at Shibe Park. In his final at-bat in the ninth inning, Gehrig launched a shot to deep center field that narrowly missed being number five. That year, the Yankees were back on top, sweeping the Cubs in four for the championship. The Yankees finished second from 1933 to 1935, but in 1934, Gehrig achieved the batting Triple Crown by leading the league in home runs (49), RBIs (165) and batting average (.363).

Though Gehrig and Ruth would be a terrific tandem through 1934, because of Ruth's outsize personality, Gehrig was often overshadowed. Still, baseball history regards him as the greatest first baseman ever. In his career, he hit 493 home runs and had a .340 batting average. He was a member of six World Series winning teams. Yet Gehrig always played in Ruth's enormous shadow.. Gehrig batted fourth in the powerful Yankees batting order (hence, he wore No. 4), protecting Ruth in the lineup (who batted third, hence, the Babe wore No. 3). His homers didn't fly quite as high or as far. Because he played second fiddle to Ruth, Gehrig's offensive exploits are often overlooked. For example, when Gehrig blasted four home runs in the 1928 World Series, Ruth made history by whacking three in one game for the second time in his career.

When it was suggested that Gehrig try to be more colorful, he said: "I'm not a headline guy. I knew that as long as I was following Babe to the plate I could have stood on my head and no one would have noticed the difference. When the Babe was through swinging, whether he hit one or fanned, nobody paid any attention to the next hitter. They all were talking about what the Babe had done."

By 1935 Babe Ruth was no longer a Yankee, but 1936 brought the arrival of Joe DiMaggio, who helped Gehrig and the Yankees win World Series titles in 1936, 1937, and 1938. The Yankees won the 1939 World Series, too, but without Gehrig. He had been diagnosed with amyotrophic lateral sclerosis, forever after known as Lou Gehrig's disease. It was incurable and fatal. He died two years later at the age of thirty-seven.

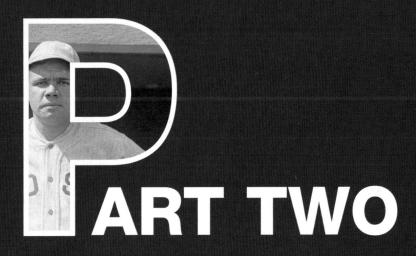

PART TWO

THE BRONX BOMBERS

Tony Lazzeri trots home after hitting a home run against the Red Sox at Fenway Park, April 24, 1937. (Courtesy of the Boston Public Library, Leslie Jones Collection)

1936

Poosh 'Em Up Tony

In the greatest run-producing day in American League history, Tony Lazzeri drove in a league record 11 runs in a 25-2 victory over the Philadelphia Athletics at Shibe Park, on May 24, 1936. The Yankees' second baseman became the first player to club two grand slam home runs in one game. Lazzeri also hit a third homer and a triple. A day earlier, Lazzeri had three homers and five runs batted in during a doubleheader sweep, giving him an incredible six home runs and 16 RBI in a three-game span.

Lazzeri, who played twelve years for the Yankees from 1926 to 1937, was the greatest second baseman in team history. He drove in 100 runs seven times and won five World Series rings. He hit .300 or better five times. In 1929, he hit a career-high .354. His reputation for driving in clutch runs earned him the nickname "Poosh 'Em Up" Tony. In the 1928 World Series sweep of the St. Louis Cardinals, he doubled and scored the eventual winning run in the clinching game, and in the 1932 World Series he finished off the Chicago Cubs with two home runs in the clinching Game 4 victory. In the 1936 Series against the Giants, won by the Yankees, Lazzeri hit a grand slam in Game 2 off Giants' pitcher Dick Coffman; it was only the second grand slam ever hit in Series competition.

Despite his reputation for timely hitting, Lazzeri is most remembered for striking out in Game 7 of the 1926 World Series. The Cardinals were leading the Yankees by a score of 3-2 in the seventh inning of the seventh game at Yankee Stadium, but starting pitcher Jess Haines was having trouble controlling his knuckle ball. In the seventh, Combs singled, Koenig bunted out, Ruth walked intentionally, Meusel grounded out, and Gehrig walked, loading the bases. With Lazzeri, a rookie, due up next, Rogers Hornsby, the Cardinals' player-manager, decided to make a pitching change. He waved in thirty-nine-year-old Grover Cleveland Alexander, the once-great, aging pitcher who had been in baseball since 1911. There were whispers that "Ole Pete" was washed up. But Hornsby showed his faith in Alexander by naming him the starting pitcher in the sixth game. The veteran responded beautifully with a complete game. The Cardinals won a laugher, 10-2, tying the Series at three games apiece. After the game, Alexander celebrated, certain he wouldn't be called to pitch in the final game. Hornsby, however, decided to have him in the bullpen just in case.

Now, at the key moment of the Series, as the fans buzzed, Alexander methodically threw his warm-up tosses. He took his time in hopes of unnerving the rookie. The day before, Lazzeri had gone 0-for-4 against Alexander. Now Lazzeri stepped up to the plate. The first pitch was low for ball one. The second pitch was a called strike. On the next pitch, Lazzeri swung and cracked a ball deep toward the left field stands. The fans and players held their breath. "Foul ball!" cried the umpire. Alexander and the Cardinals sighed in relief. The ball was foul by inches. Lazzeri swung at Alexander's next pitch and missed for strike three. Baseball fans talked about Lazzeri's strikeout for years. When Alexander went into the Hall of Fame in 1938, Lazzeri was still an active player, but he earned the distinction of being the only player to have his name on someone else's Hall of Fame plaque. That's because Alexander's plaque, in part, reads, "He won the 1926 world championship for the Cardinals by striking out Lazzeri with the bases full in the final crisis."

The popular Lazzeri was a hero in the Italian American communities around the United States. He helped draw thousands of newly arrived immigrants to ballparks and helped foster an interest in baseball in many of America's newest citizens. Manager Miller Huggins called him the type of player that comes along "once in a generation." Known as a quiet leader, Lazzeri suffered from epilepsy, although he was never affected by the disorder during a game. In 1946, he died of a heart attack, likely induced by a seizure, at age forty-three. In 1991, Lazzeri was elected to the Hall of Fame and finally received a well-deserved bronze plaque of his own.

CYCLE HITTER

A player is said to "hit for the cycle" when he hits a single, double, triple, and home run in the same game, though not necessarily in that order. Collecting the hits in that order is known as a natural cycle. This feat is rare.

Tony Lazzeri achieved an amazing feat when he hit for the cycle in natural order against the Philadelphia Athletics, on June 3, 1932. Lazzeri collected a single first, a double second, a triple third and then a home run in that order—capping off his natural cycle with a grand slam home run!

Bob Meusel is the first American League player to hit for the cycle three times. A member of the famed Murderer's Row Yankees, Meusel teamed with Babe Ruth and Earle Combs to form one of the best outfields in baseball history. He batted over .300 seven times and, in 1925, led the American League with 33 home runs and 134 runs batted in.

Yankees Hitting for the Cycle		
Player	Opponent	Date
Bert Daniels	Chicago	July 25, 1912
Bob Meusel	@ Washington	May 7, 1921
Bob Meusel	@ Philadelphia	July 3, 1922
Bob Meusel	@ Detroit	July 26, 1928
Tony Lazzeri	@ Philadelphia	June 3, 1932
Lou Gehrig	Chicago	June 25, 1934
Joe DiMaggio	Washington	July 9, 1937
Lou Gehrig	St. Louis	August 1, 1937
Buddy Rosar	Cleveland	July 19, 1940
Joe Gordon	@ Boston	September 8, 1940
Joe DiMaggio	@ Chicago	May 20, 1948
Mickey Mantle	Chicago	July 23, 1957
Bobby Murcer	Texas	August 29, 1972
Tony Fernandez	Oakland	September 3, 1995
Melky Cabrera	@ Chicago	August 2, 2009

Part Two

1937

DiMaggio Breaks Out

Babe Ruth was the king of baseball during the Roaring Twenties, but by 1935, he had retired from the game. Not to worry, Yankee fans, for the Bronx Bombers were reloading and building a new dynasty to dominate through the end of the decade. Ammunition arrived in 1936 in the form of Joe DiMaggio. The shy, soft-spoken center fielder hit .323 his rookie season, with 29 home runs and 125 runs batted in. First baseman Lou Gehrig, a holdover from the great Yankee teams of the 1920s, batted a sparkling .354 with an American League-leading 49 homers and 152 RBI. The Yankees bludgeoned their opponents, winning 102 regular season games, and sprinted past the other teams in the standings as if the opponent were standing still, winning the American League pennant by 19½ games over their next closest rival. In the first Subway Series since 1923 and the Yankees' first fall classic without the Babe, the Bronx Bombers whipped the New York Giants in six games. DiMaggio banged out nine hits, including three doubles, and drove in three runs. It was the start of a record-setting Yankees winning streak.

The Yankees used 1936 as a springboard to an unprecedented four consecutive World Series victories. A lineup that included Gehrig, DiMaggio, second baseman Tony Lazzeri, shortstop Frank Crosetti, third baseman Red Rolfe, catcher Bill Dickey and outfielders George Selkirk and Jake Powell supported a pitching staff that featured Red Ruffing, Lefty Gomez and Monte Pearson. Outfielders Tommy Henrich and Charlie Keller arrived in 1937 and 1939, respectively. Joe Gordon replaced Lazzeri in 1938.

The Yankees were good enough in 1937 to win 102 regular season games for the second straight season, this time romping to a 13-game bulge in the pennant chase. The Yankees again made short work of the Giants in the World Series, this time needing only five games to defeat the crosstown rivals. Gehrig enjoyed his last productive season, batting .351 with 37 homers and 158 RBI. DiMaggio enjoyed an otherworldly campaign, batting .346 with a league-leading 46 homers and 167 RBI. Dickey finished at .332 and smacked 29 homers

Part Two

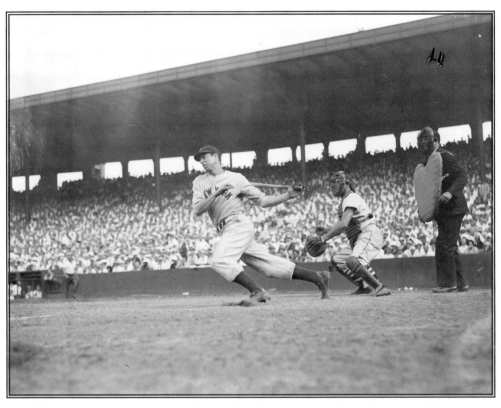

Joe DiMaggio connecting in front of Boston Red Sox catcher Johnny Peacock at Fenway Park, 1941. (Courtesy of the Boston Public Library, Leslie Jones Collection)

and 133 RBI. The Yankees also had the American League's only two 20-game winners in lefty Gomez and righty Ruffing and a standout relief pitcher in Johnny Murphy, who recorded 13 victories coming out of the bullpen.

Gehrig would drop off to .295 in 1938, but the Yankees were still good enough to reach 99 wins and another World Series appearance. This time, led by pitchers Ruffing, Gomez, Pearson, and Spud Chandler, the two-time defending world champion Yankees swept their opponent, the Chicago Cubs, in four games, in the process becoming the first team to win three straight World Series titles.

For the Yankees, 1939 was business as usual, winning 106 games and the pennant by 17 games. DiMaggio batted .381 to lead the American League, and captured the first of his three Most Valuable Player awards. The Yankees won their fourth consecutive World Series by sweeping the Cincinnati Reds. In an incredible display of domination, the Yankees had now won 13 of their last 14 Series games and 28 of their last 31 Series games.

While Yankee manager Joe McCarthy was fortunate enough to have a great collection of stars in pinstripes in the late 1930s—some called him a "push-button manager" and said that anyone could manage those great Yankees teams—Joe DiMaggio said, "Never a day went by when you didn't learn something from McCarthy." McCarthy's Yankees were practically unbeatable en route to their four championships in a row, often clinching the pennant in early September, a month before the season ended, and then crushing all opposition in the World Series. But Joe McCarthy was not a "push-button manager," for it takes great skill to handle a large group of talented ball players. It isn't easy to keep them happy and to keep them winning. As for the ball players, they need more than mechanical ability to win consistently. It takes spirit, unselfishness, and courage. The team captain, Lou Gehrig, above all others personified those qualities.

McCarthy shared a special bond with Gehrig, whom he called "the finest example of a ballplayer, sportsman, and citizen that baseball has ever known." When Gehrig decided on May 2, 1936, to end his incredible streak of 2,130 consecutive games played, he told his manager, McCarthy, he wanted to sit down "for the good of the team" and his boss reluctantly complied with the request. At the tearful testimonial held in Gehrig's honor on July 4, 1939, McCarthy told Gehrig, "Lou, what else can I say except that it was a sad day in the life of everybody who knew you when you told me you were quitting as a ballplayer because you felt yourself a hindrance to the team. My God, man, you were never that."

Three Yankees were on the 1937 All Star team. Left to right: Lou Gehrig, Joe Cronin, Bill Dickey, Joe DiMaggio, Charley Gehringer, Jimmie Foxx, and Hank Greenberg, at Griffith Stadium in Washington, D.C. July 7, 1937. (Harris & Ewing Collection, Library of Congress)

Joe McCarthy (l) helping to raise the flag at the Yankees' season opener in Washington, April 21, 1939. This would be Lou Gehrig's final season. (Harris & Ewing Collection, Library of Congress)

Without Gehrig, the mantle of leadership fell on DiMaggio's shoulders and he wore it well in 1940, again pacing the team and leading the American League with a .352 batting average and 133 runs batted in. This time, however, the Bronx Bombers fell short. In a tight three-team race, it was the Detroit Tigers who won the pennant; the Yankees finished in third place, two games off the pace. It was a shocking finish for a franchise with high expectations, and left historians to wonder what might have been. As the Yanks would come to see by finishing first in 1941, 1942, and 1943, a pennant in 1940 would have meant eight consecutive pennants flying over Yankee Stadium, a feat without precedent, and one that even today would leave us breathless.

SCORING MACHINE

Red Rolfe set the major league record by scoring at least one run in 18 consecutive games from August 9 to 25, 1939. (Kenny Lofton of the Cleveland Indians equaled the record in 2000.) Although a stomach ulcer caused him to play most of his career in pain, Rolfe helped lead the Yankees to six pennants and five World Series championships in his seven years as the regular third baseman from 1935 to 1941. A reliable leadoff batter, Rolfe hit over .300 four times, including a career-high .329 in 1939, when he had his best season ever, leading the American League in hits (213), doubles (46), and runs scored (139). He scored at least 100 runs seven seasons in a row.

"The Luckiest Man"

Lou Gehrig became known as "the Iron Horse" for setting a record of playing in the most consecutive games. The streak began on June 1, 1925, when Gehrig came into a game as a pinch hitter. The next day, regular first baseman Wally Pipp sat out a game with a headache and Gehrig started in his place. Gehrig did not leave the Yankees starting lineup for the next fourteen years. The Yankee captain played in 2,130 consecutive games. The record stood until 1995, when Cal Ripken Jr. played in his 2,131st straight game for the Baltimore Orioles.

Gehrig himself ended the streak on May 2, 1939, when he told his manager Joe McCarthy not to play him in Detroit because he was tired. Gehrig would never play again. Gehrig had taken himself out of the lineup "for the good of the team." The Yankees first baseman knew that something was wrong. A lifetime .340 hitter, Gehrig had slumped to .295 in 1938 and was batting a miserable .143 through the 1939 season's first eight games. After a teammate applauded him for making a simple putout at first base, Gehrig knew it was time to sit down. "When guys start feeling sorry for you . . ." he said.

Two months later, he was diagnosed with amyotrophic lateral sclerosis (ALS), an incurable neurological disease. It points up Gehrig's stature, not only in baseball but also in the national spotlight, that ALS would come to be known as "Lou Gehrig's Disease."

To express their admiration, the Yankees designated the doubleheader against the Washington Senators as "Lou Gehrig Appreciation Day." On the Fourth of July 1939, Gehrig's teammates, past and present, including Babe Ruth and all of the members of the superb 1927 team, as well as 61,808 fans, came to honor the man they called "the Pride of the Yankees."

The tribute between games of the doubleheader lasted for more than forty minutes. There were speeches by Mayor Fiorello La Guardia and Postmaster James A. Farley. Each of the many dignitaries on the field spoke in glowing terms of their stricken former teammate. It was as if Gehrig, in the words of sports columnist Paul Gallico, was "present at his own funeral." Gehrig, never one to seek the spotlight, stood with head bowed, hands placed deep into the rear pockets of his uniform pants, scratching at the turf with his spikes.

After being showered with gifts and praise, it was finally Gehrig's turn to speak. The crowd chanted, "We want Lou. We want Lou." He was so shaken with emotion that at first it appeared he would not be able to talk at all. The Yankee Stadium crowd, sitting in absolute silence, watched as the Iron Horse, obviously sick and walking with a slight hitch in his gait, approached the microphone. Although he probably knew he was dying, Lou said he considered himself a lucky man with a lot to live for. When Gehrig finished speaking, Ruth threw his arms around the big first baseman and hugged him. Gehrig's sincere, humbled words and Ruth's impulsive show of affection brought tears to many pairs of eyes.

At season's end the Yankees retired Gehrig's number 4, making his the first retired number in sports. (Since then, over one hundred numbers have been retired.) To this day Gehrig is the only Yankees player ever to wear the number. The Hall of Fame, whose building opened earlier this same year, in Cooperstown, New York, waived its five-year eligibility requirement for Gehrig. Instead of having to wait the mandated five years after retiring to be eligible, Gehrig was voted into the Hall of Fame immediately. He died two years later, on June 2, 1941, at his home in the Riverdale section of the Bronx. He was thirty-seven years old.

GEHRIG'S FAREWELL SPEECH

There are those who believe Lou Gehrig knew he was dying as he spoke at Yankee Stadium on that memorable day. If this is true, his brief speech points out the selflessness and bravery of the man. He said simply:

"Fans, for the past two weeks you have been reading about the bad break I got. Yet today I consider myself the luckiest man on the face of this earth. I have been in ballparks for seventeen years and have never received anything but kindness and encouragement from you fans.

"Look at these grand men. Which of you wouldn't consider it the highlight of his career just to associate with them for even one day? Sure, I'm lucky. Who wouldn't consider it an honor to have known Jacob Ruppert? Also, the builder of baseball's greatest empire, Ed Barrow? To have spent six years with that wonderful little fellow, Miller Huggins? Then to have spent the next nine years with that outstanding leader, that smart student of psychology, the best manager in baseball today, Joe McCarthy? Sure, I'm lucky.

"When the New York Giants, a team you would give your right arm to beat, and vice versa, sends you a gift—that's something. When everybody down to the groundskeepers and those boys in white coats remember you with trophies— that's something. When you have a wonderful mother-in-law who takes sides with you in squabbles with her own daughter—that's something. When you have a father and a mother who work all their lives so you can have an education and build your body—it's a blessing. When you have a wife who has been a tower of strength and shown more courage than you dreamed existed—that's the finest I know.

"So I close in saying that I may have had a tough break, but I have an awful lot to live for."

1941
Joe DiMaggio's Hitting Streak

Of all the legendary Yankees batting records that once seemed unconquerable—Babe Ruth's 714 career home runs and Roger Maris's 61 home runs in a season—only Joe DiMaggio's hitting streak in 1941 has stood the test of time. "Joltin' Joe" hit safely in 56 games in a row. The closest anybody has come to matching DiMaggio's feat is a 44-game hitting streak by Pete Rose in 1978.

DiMaggio began the incredible streak with a single against the Chicago White Sox, on May 15, 1941. A DiMaggio base hit was no surprise. Having won batting titles in 1939 and 1940, baseball fans were used to seeing him hit safely. DiMaggio got a hit in the next game, and in the next, and in the game after that. Pretty soon he had strung together a lengthy hitting streak. Over the next two months, he would get at least one base hit in every game in which he played.

Newspapermen covering the Yankees flocked to the centerfielder's locker after he set the club record of 29 games in a row, on June 16. DiMaggio has said he became conscious of the streak when it stretched to 25 straight games on June 10. Amid the hubbub, the unflappable DiMaggio never changed expression, perhaps because of his impressive 61-game streak as an eighteen-year old playing for the San Francisco Seals of the Pacific Coast League (a rung beneath the major leagues) in 1933.

"The Yankee Clipper" broke Rogers Hornsby's National League mark of 33 straight games, on June 21. The next record to fall was George Sisler's single-season mark of 41 consecutive games with a hit, on June 29, against the Washington Senators. Official scorers admitted to feeling the pressure (they didn't want to end or prolong the streak on a questionable play). The final standing mark was shattered on July 2 when DiMaggio passed Willie Keeler's major-league record of 44 games, set in 1897.

DiMaggio's streak reached 50 games on July 11, pounding out four hits against the St. Louis Browns. On July 16, he got three hits off two Cleveland pitchers, Al Milnar and Joe Krakauskas, marking game No. 56. The sensational streak finally ended on July 17, 1941, before 67,468 people in Cleveland's Municipal Stadium. Indians left-hander Al Smith retired DiMaggio on two hard smashes to third baseman Ken Keltner, who made two outstanding plays to rob potential hits. DiMaggio walked in his second plate appearance. Coming up for the last time against a knuckleballer, Jim Bagby, with two out and a man on first, DiMaggio needed a hit to keep the streak going. DiMaggio rapped a Babgy pitch at shortstop Lou Boudreau who threw to start a double play. The streak had ended at 56 games. During that time, DiMaggio had 91 hits and batted .408 with 15 home runs and fifty-five runs batted in—not a bad season for some players.

Part Two

Joe DiMaggio kissing his bat during "The Streak" in 1941. (The Sporting News Pub. Co., Library of Congress)

An undeterred DiMaggio remained hot. He hit safely in the next 16 games, making his streak 72 out of 73 games. He w on the Most Valuable Player award that year, beating out Ted Williams in a season in which Williams batted over .400. For the season, DiMaggio batted .357 with 30 homers and a league-leading 125 runs batted in.

The summer of 1941 belonged to Joe DiMaggio, even though baseball was merely a footnote to world events. President Franklin Delano Roosevelt had warned the nation of Hitler's plan to extend his Nazi domination to the western hemisphere. To receive the latest news, people flocked to radios and newspapers. Soon the entire nation was also checking DiMaggio's performance in the morning papers and getting radio bulletins on every at-bat. DiMaggio was more than a baseball idol. He was a national celebrity. A song called *Joltin' Joe DiMaggio*, lyrics by Alan Courtney and performed by Les Brown and his Orchestra, with Betty Bonney on vocals, hit Number 12 on the pop charts in 1941.

Led by DiMaggio, the Yankees won the World Series in 1941. In all, he played on nine World Series winning teams. He won three MVP awards (1939, 1941, and 1947), and was elected to the Hall of Fame in 1955. DiMaggio was especially a hero in the Italian American community and he remained a beloved national celebrity until his death in 1999 at the age of eighty-four.

JOLTIN' JOE

(Bowman Gum, via Wikimedia Commons)

At his peak, Joe DiMaggio was often saluted in the popular culture. In addition to being serenaded in song as *Joltin' Joe DiMaggio* by Les Brown, he was immortalized in print by Ernest Hemingway in *The Old Man and the Sea* when the main character Santiago says, "I would like to take the great DiMaggio fishing; maybe he was as poor as we are and would understand."

DiMaggio was also mentioned in films and Broadway shows; the sailors in *South Pacific* sing that Bloody Mary's skin is "tender as DiMaggio's glove." Years later, he was remembered in song by Paul Simon, who wondered: "Where have you gone, Joe DiMaggio? Our nation turns its lonely eyes to you. What's that you say, Mrs. Robinson, Joltin' Joe has left and gone away."

The song *Mrs. Robinson*, written by Paul Simon and performed by Simon and Garfunkel, won the Grammy Award for Record of the Year in 1969. The reference to DiMaggio is "one of the most well-known lines that I've ever written," says Simon, who grew up a fan of Mickey Mantle. When asked why Mantle wasn't mentioned in the song instead of DiMaggio, Simon explained that the number of syllables in DiMaggio's name fit the beat.

For his part, DiMaggio, sensitive to any derogatory public comment that could affect his legacy, was puzzled by Simon's lyric, saying he hadn't gone anywhere, and sought an answer to the meaning of the song when he and Simon were dining at the same New York restaurant. Only when Simon explained his motives to express a feeling that true heroes are a thing of the past, and that the line was meant as a sincere tribute to DiMaggio's grace and dignity, was DiMaggio mollified.

When DiMaggio died in 1999, Simon performed *Mrs. Robinson* at Yankee Stadium in DiMaggio's honor.

1941

The Missed Third Strike

The 1941 World Series was a match-up pitting one experienced World Series team against an upstart in the Fall Classic. For the American League, Joe McCarthy's Yankees were making their fifth appearance in six years. But the National Leaguers, Leo Durocher's Brooklyn Dodgers, hadn't been in the Series since 1920.

The subway rivals—Brooklyn is one of New York's five boroughs, as is the home borough of the Yankees, the Bronx—were evenly matched, and the first three October games were each decided by one run. The Yankees took the first game 3-2, on Red Ruffing's six-hitter and a Joe Gordon home run. The Dodgers claimed Game Two by the same score behind a complete-game effort from Whitlow Wyatt. New York caught a break in Game Three. Brooklyn's Freddie Fitzsimmons and New York's Marius Russo were locked in a scoreless tie when, with two outs in the seventh inning, Russo hit a line drive that struck Fitzsimmons on the knee. Shortstop Pee Wee Reese caught the deflected ball in the air for the third out, but the injured Fitzsimmons was replaced by Dodgers relief ace Hugh Casey. The Yankees scored twice in the eighth inning against Casey to win the third game 2-1.

Game four, played in Ebbets Field, Brooklyn, is one that lingers in the memory of New York sports fans. Through eight innings of another tense battle, Brooklyn clung to a 4-3 lead, thanks to pinch-hitter Jimmy Wasdell's two-run double and Pete Reiser's two-run homer. Casey had taken the mound again, and the reliever had shut down the Yankees from the fifth inning through the eighth. Casey promptly retired Johnny Sturm and Red Rolfe on ground balls for the first two Yankee outs in the ninth inning. With three balls and two strikes on New York's Tommy Henrich, the crowd stood in anticipation of a victory by the hometown Dodgers, which would have tied the series at two games apiece. Brooklyn catcher Mickey Owen signaled for a curveball. The pitch fooled the batter completely. Henrich, a New York outfielder, swung and missed, and umpire Larry Goetz signaled a strikeout.

Unfortunately, the pitch fooled Owens as well. The ball glanced off his mitt and shot back to the wall. If a pitch gets past the catcher on a third strike, the batter is allowed to run to first base—and that's just what Henrich did. The next man up, Joe DiMaggio, singled to left, and Charlie Keller put the Yankees ahead with a two-run double. The pitcher Casey was coming undone. After a walk to Bill Dickey, he yielded another two-run double to Joe Gordon. The Yankees' Johnny Murphy then pitched one scoreless inning of relief and New York handed Brooklyn a devastating defeat, 7-4. The next day, Ernie Bonham put the Dodgers out of their misery by tossing a four-hitter, and helped by Henrich's homer, the Yankees trampled the Dodgers 3-1 in Game Five to win the title.

"That was a tough break for poor Mickey to get," said Henrich. "I bet he feels like a nickel's worth of dog meat."

Owen's miscue had let a potential Series-tying victory get away, and had given the Yankees new life. Owen couldn't forgive himself for opening the door. "Sure, it was my fault," Owen said after the game. "The ball was a low curve that broke down. It hit the edge of my glove and glanced off, but I should have had him out anyway."

"It was as good a curveball as Casey ever threw," he added. "I should have had it."

1943

Dickey Soldiers On

Bill Dickey was one of the best all-around catchers in major league baseball history. He was known as a great handler of pitchers, and as a durable iron-man that played a key role on dominant title teams. As a player, Dickey's New York Yankees went to the World Series eight times and won seven championships. Legendary sports writer Dan Daniel once wrote of Dickey: "He isn't just a catcher, he's a ball club. He isn't just a player, he's an influence."

Dickey was the foundation of a Yankees dynasty. His playing career extended from 1928 to 1946, bridging the Babe Ruth and Lou Gehrig era to the Joe DiMaggio era. As Gehrig's roommate, Dickey was the first Yankee to find out about Gehrig's illness. Dickey also managed the Yankees in 1946, and mentored a young catcher named Yogi Berra. He completed his connection to the dynasty as a coach with the team throughout the 1950s in the Mickey Mantle era.

As a rookie in 1928, Dickey tried to impress manager Miller Huggins with his home run swing. Huggins explained to him that a team with power hitters such as Ruth and Gehrig didn't need another home run threat. What Huggins wanted was for Dickey to be consistent behind the plate and in the batter's box. And that's exactly what the young catcher would provide.

One of the finest hitting catchers of all time, Dickey batted .300 or better in eleven different seasons. His best was in 1936, when he hit .362 and drove in 107 runs in just 112 games, and in 1937, when he hit .332 with 29 homers and 133 RBI in 140 games. An excellent judge of the strike zone, Dickey struck out only 289 times in 6,300 at bats, including the 1935 season when he struck out just eleven times. Few players enjoyed a home field advantage like Dickey, who hit 135 of his 202 career homers (66.8 percent) at Yankee Stadium.

Defensively, he set a record by catching at least 100 games for 13 seasons in a row, a mark that wasn't equaled until Johnny Bench accomplished it in the 1970s. Dickey led AL

Bill Dickey on the steps at Fenway Park in 1937. (Courtesy of the Boston Public Library, Leslie Jones Collection)

catchers in assists three times and putouts six times. In 1931, he became the first catcher to play an entire season without allowing a passed ball. He was the American League's starting catcher in six of the first eight All Star games, and was selected as an All Star eleven times.

"Dickey was the heart of the team defensively and commanded tremendous respect from the Yankee pitchers," said teammate Billy Werber. "Once the game started, he ran the show."

No catcher has caught more World Series games than Bill Dickey (38), and he caught every inning of those games he played in. Dickey wasn't just along for the ride, of course. He hit .438 in the 1932 World Series, went 4 for 4 in Game 1 of the 1938 Series, and drove in at least one run in each game of the 1939 Series. But his biggest October moment came in the fifth game of the 1943 World Series—with the Yankees minus the great DiMaggio away on military duty—when Dickey broke a scoreless battle in the sixth inning with a two-run home run against the St. Louis Cardinals that spurred the Yankees to another title, Dickey's last as a player.

Dickey was drafted for military service on June 3, 1944, even though he was thirty-seven years old and suffering from a sinus condition. He was sworn in with the U.S. Naval Reserve, attaining the rank of Lieutenant Junior Grade, and served as an athletic officer at a Navy Hospital in Hawaii. There he managed the U.S. Navy team that won the 1944 Army-Navy Service World Series.

Dickey was back with the Yankees in 1946 and succeeded Joe McCarthy as the club's manager in May, though he didn't return the following season. He returned in 1949 as a Yankees coach under manager Casey Stengel and helped teach Yogi Berra to be a great catcher. As a coach, Dickey was credited with teaching Berra, an awkward receiver, the basic skills of catching. "Bill is learnin' me his experience," said Berra, who became an excellent fielder and Hall of Famer.

The Yankees have retired the uniform No. 8 worn by both Dickey and Berra. On August 21, 1988, a plaque honoring Dickey, along with one of Berra, was placed in Monument Park at Yankee Stadium that recognized Dickey as "First in Line of Great Yankee Catchers. The Epitome of Yankee Pride." After his induction into the Hall of Fame in 1954, Dickey declared the honor, "the nicest thing ever to happen to me."

1947

One Out From Immortality

The 1947 World Series featured baseball's most popular player, the New York Yankees' Joe DiMaggio, and its man of the hour, the Brooklyn Dodgers' Jackie Robinson. This was the year when the Dodgers introduced Robinson as the first African-American player in modern-day major league history. But this wild, six-game Fall Classic wound up being dominated by virtual no-names.

These Yankees were no Bronx Bombers, as no player knocked in 100 runs and only one, DiMaggio, belted more than 20 home runs. The '47 Yanks won with great pitching from Allie Reynolds, Spud Chandler, rookie Spec Shea, and reliever Joe Page. Yet in the World Series, the Yankees came out swinging, winning the first two games, 5-3 and 10-3. In the opener, Dodgers' starter Ralph Branca pitched four perfect innings before the Yankees exploded to score all five runs in the fifth inning. The rookie Shea was credited with the win but needed four innings of relief help from Page. The Yankees banged out 15 hits in the second game as Reynolds coasted to a complete game victory.

Back at home in Ebbets Field for game three, the Dodgers, desperately in need of a victory, took control early, scoring six runs in the second inning. New York staged a valiant comeback attempt, but the Brooklynites held on to win game three, 9-8, though a young Yankees catcher named Yogi Berra smashed the first pinch-hit home run in Series history.

The next game was the one that left fans in disbelief. Yankees starting pitcher Floyd "Bill" Bevens had a fastball like lightning, but its accuracy was always in question. Bevens had labored to a 7-13 record in 1947. In game four of the Series, he was at his unpredictable best—and worst. After eight innings on a cold afternoon at Ebbets Field in Brooklyn, Bevens had surrendered eight walks. But he also hadn't given up a hit, and was three outs away from becoming the first pitcher to throw a no-hitter in a World Series game. The Dodgers had scored once in the fifth inning (on two walks, a bunt, and an infield out), but trailed 2-1 as they prepared for their last at-bat in the bottom of the ninth.

Bevens retired the first batter, catcher Bruce Edwards, on a long fly out, and then walked Carl Furillo. After a foul out by Spider Jorgensen, pinch runner Al Gionfriddo stole second base. When pinch hitter Pete Reiser came up, Bucky Harris, in his first season as the Yankees' manager, made a controversial decision by ordering Reiser be walked intentionally. It was Bevens' tenth walk, and more importantly, put the winning run on base by a free pass.

Dodgers' manager Burt Shotton then turned to pinch hitter Harry "Cookie" Lavagetto. The veteran had only 69 at-bats in 1947. With the count no balls and one strike, Lavagetto drilled the ball past right fielder Tommy Henrich. Gionfriddo scored, and so did pinch runner Eddie Miksis. With just one pitch, Bevens lost the game, the no-hitter, and the Series lead.

Instead of the Yankees taking control of the series 3 games to 1, the Series was now tied at 2 games all, and more excitement was still to come. The Yankees responded to the devastating loss by winning the next game, 2-1, as DiMaggio homered and Shea pitched a four-hitter and helped his cause by driving home a run. The American Leaguers looked to clinch the title in Game 6 at Yankee Stadium, but the National Leaguers had other ideas. Brooklyn jumped out of the gate strong by scoring four early runs, but by the fourth inning the Yankees had gained the lead, 5-4. In the sixth inning, the Dodgers went back ahead with a four-run rally, capped by Pee Wee Reese's two-run single.

The Yankees made a bid to tie the score in the bottom of the sixth inning against the Dodgers' starter Joe Hatten, a 17-game winner that season. Joe DiMaggio strolled to the plate to face the left-hander. The Yankees were trailing 8-5 with two outs and two runners on base. DiMaggio smashed the ball 415 feet toward the left-centerfield bullpen at Yankee Stadium, but Al Gionfriddo—a defensive replacement just inserted into the game as a pinch runner by Dodgers' manager Burt Shotton—made a spectacular, twisting game-saving catch at the wall. A frustrated DiMaggio, in a rare public display of emotion, kicked at the dirt over his disappointment, correctly sensing this dramatic blow would be the Yanks' last hurrah of the day. As it turned out, Brooklyn held on for an 8-6 victory to even the series at three games apiece.

The momentum seemed to stay with the Dodgers in the deciding seventh game as Shotton's troops took a 2-0 lead and knocked out Shea in the second inning. But the Yankees fought back to take the lead in the fourth inning, and bolstered by impressive relief pitching from Joe Page, who shut down the Dodgers over the final five innings, the Yankees held on for a 5-2 victory and another world championship triumph.

The strangest twist to this wacky Series was that the three most memorable performers—Bevens, Lavagetto, and Gionfriddo—were all playing their last professional games.

1949

Yankees Steal a Pennant

In 1949, manager Casey Stengel's Yankees clung to first place despite a series of injuries to key players and all the while with the surging Boston Red Sox hot on their heels. New York's star centerfielder, Joe DiMaggio, was never the same player after the war. Injuries followed DiMaggio throughout his career after he returned from the Army. In 1947, a bone spur was removed from his left heel. The next year, he developed one in his right heel, but he played through the pain, telling a teammate it was "like having a nail in your heel." By 1949 his career seemed to be over. He couldn't stand on the heel without pain, and he missed the first 65 games of the season. But on June 28 the pain suddenly went away just in time for a three-game series in Boston. In one of the greatest comebacks in baseball history, DiMaggio hit four home runs, had nine runs batted in, and made thirteen catches in the outfield in the series. The Yankees won all three games to keep hold of first place.

Juggling the lineup to keep his players fresh, Stengel somehow kept the team in a tight pennant race. On the last day of the season, the Red Sox were in New York to play a doubleheader against the Yankees. The Red Sox held a one game lead. If the Yanks could win both games they would take the flag. Boston's Ted Williams was having another great year. The Sox's two best pitchers, Ellis Kinder and Mel Parnell, were rested and ready for the Yanks. But the Yankees upset all the odds. They won the two games and the pennant. In the first game, after trailing 4-0, the Yankees stormed back to beat Parnell, 5-4, when Johnny Lindell hit an eighth inning homer to complete a Yankees comeback. In the second game, the Bombers withstood a late Sox rally to hold on for a 5-3 win. Afterward, a humble Stengel said, "I couldn't have done it without my players."

DiMaggio, playing in only 76 games, finished the season with 67 runs batted in. The Yankees went on to face the Brooklyn Dodgers for the world championship. The first two games of the Yankees-Dodgers World Series were as tight as the pennant race, and the series opener was one for the ages. Allie Reynolds and Don Newcombe waged a scoreless duel through eight innings, with the two powerful teams combining for just six hits. When Reynolds retired the Dodgers in order in the ninth inning, on any normal day that would have concluded a brilliant two-hit shutout. But because Newcombe was just as stingy, the Yankees still needed a run to win. They sent first baseman Tommy Henrich up to lead off the ninth against Newcombe, who had already struck out 11 batters. Broadcaster Mel Allen always liked to call Henrich "Ol' Reliable" for his ability to deliver in clutch situations. Henrich did just that against Newcombe, slugging a solo homer over the short right field porch for a walk-off blast, the first in World Series history. The Dodgers won the second game by the same score of 1-0 on a double by Jackie Robinson and a single by Gil Hodges. Then the Yankees won the next three games at Ebbets Field to give Casey Stengel his first World Series championship. It was just a hint of great things to come.

Tommy Henrich, left, New York Yankees first baseman, and pitcher Allie Reynolds in the locker room at Yankee Stadium on October 5, 1949. In the first game of the 1949 World Series, Reynolds pitched a two-hit, shut-out ball game against the Dodgers, while Henrich delivered a ninth-inning home run that gave the Yankees a 1-0 win. (AP Photo)

HAIL THE CHIEF

In 1951, Allie Reynolds became the first American League pitcher to record two no-hitters in the same season. The first no-hitter was on July 12, in Cleveland, against Bob Feller and the Indians. Gene Woodling hit a home run in the top of the seventh inning for the only run of the game. Then, on September 28, at Yankee Stadium, Reynolds was one out away from joining Johnny Vander Meer of the National League's Cincinnati Reds as the only pitchers to that point to accomplish the feat twice in a season. That final out was Ted Williams of the Boston Red Sox-one of the best hitters of all-time—and Reynolds had to get him out twice. Williams hit a foul pop-up that catcher Yogi Berra dropped. Unfazed, on the very next pitch, Reynolds got Williams to hit another foul pop-up, and this time Berra squeezed the ball in his mitt for the final out.

Reynolds, known as The Chief because he was one-quarter Creek Indian, pitched eight seasons for the Yankees from 1947 to 1954, and still ranks in the team's all-time Top 10 in wins (131, 10th), win-loss percentage (.686, 9th), and shutouts (27, 5th).

PART THREE

MICKEY, CASEY, WHITEY, AND YOGI

Mickey Mantle hit balls high and far, from both sides of the plate. (AP Photo)

1953

Mantle's Tape Measure Homers

Part Three

Mickey Mantle could hit a baseball as far as anyone. Legendary sluggers like Babe Ruth, Jimmie Foxx and Hank Greenberg all hit the ball for great distances, yet the era of the "tape-measure" homer didn't arrive until Mantle did. His longest home run on record was a 565-foot clout hit at old Griffith Stadium on April 17, 1953. Mantle, a switch-hitter for the New York Yankees, was batting right-handed against left-handed pitcher Chuck Stobbs of the Washington Senators. Mantle hit a rising line drive that nicked the lower right-hand corner of a huge beer sign atop a football scoreboard behind the left-centerfield bleachers. The ball left the stadium, carried across a street and landed in the back yard of a home.

This blow was responsible for the expression "tape-measure home run" because the Yankees publicity director, Red Patterson, immediately left the press box, found himself a tape measure and paced off the distance to the spot where witnesses said the ball came down.

Mantle and perhaps others probably have hit longer home runs. That was certainly the view of Stobbs.

"He hit 'em pretty far against a lot of people," said Stobbs. "The only reason they remember this one is because they marked the spot on the beer sign where the ball left the park, but Bucky Harris [the Senators' manager] later made them take the marker down.

"I got Mantle out pretty good later on," added Stobbs. "I think he was 2 for 25 off me one year, but nobody ever talks about that."

One of Mantle's 52 homers in 1956, his 19th of the season, blasted on May 30, carried special significance. It came within 18 inches of becoming the only fair ball ever hit out of Yankee Stadium. Hitting left-handed against Pedro Ramos of the Washington Senators with two men on base in the fifth inning, Mantle hit a mammoth drive to right field that struck just below the cornice high above the third deck. Ever since Yankee Stadium was built in 1923, nobody had ever come close to hitting that copper filigree. Mantle hit it, some 525 feet away. There is no telling how far the ball might have traveled had it managed those 18 inches to clear the façade, but the ball would likely have wound up nearly 600 feet away from its starting point.

Yankees fans had become accustomed to the Mick's power, but on May 22, 1963, Mantle nearly put a ball into orbit. The Yankees were hosting the lowly Kansas City Athletics, so less than 10,000 fans were on hand to witness the Bombers edge the A's in extra innings. With the score tied 7-7 in the bottom of the 11th inning, Mantle faced Kansas City right-hander Bill Fischer. Batting left-handed, Mantle laced a 2-2 pitch that hit the upper-deck façade in right field while still rising. The Yankees won, but all everyone could talk about was Mantle's shot, estimated at 535 feet. It was the Mick's fourth-longest homer, but Mantle himself said, "It's the hardest ball I ever hit left-handed."

Mantle's longest home run batting left-handed traveled 560 feet. He hit it off Paul Foytack of the Detroit Tigers, on September 10, 1960; the blast cleared the right-field roof at Briggs Stadium and landed across Trumbull Avenue. Mantle liked to hit against the Tigers at Briggs Stadium. Four years earlier, on June 20, 1956, batting right-handed off Detroit's Billy Hoeft, he hit a towering fly ball that cleared the center-field fence at the 440-foot mark and landed 525 feet away. Two and a half months later, he belted a ball 550 feet batting right-handed off Billy Pierce of the Chicago White Sox, which cleared the left-field roof at Comiskey Park, on September 18, 1956.

1953

Five-Peat

When the New York Yankees finished in third place in 1948, the owners of the team fired manager Bucky Harris. The Yankees were used to finishing first, so no one was surprised that Harris was let go. But the appointment of Casey Stengel as the new manager was shocking.

Charles Dillon Stengel had acquired the nickname Casey because he was from Kansas City (or K.C.). Because Casey would achieve such success as a Yankees manager, many people don't realize he had a 14-year playing career from 1912 to 1925. Casey had been a fair major league ballplayer. In his first game with the Brooklyn Dodgers in 1912 he got four hits in the game. "The writers promptly declared they had seen the new Ty Cobb," said Stengel. "It took me only a few days to correct that impression." His most memorable moments on the field occurred while playing for the New York Giants in the 1923 World Series against the Yankees. Stengel won the opening game with an inside-the-park home run with two outs in the ninth inning, the first Series homer in new Yankee Stadium. Then he won Game 3 with a seventh inning home run into the right-field stands at Yankee Stadium for a thrilling 1-0 victory. But he is most remembered for entertaining fans during games. He once kept a sparrow hidden under his cap and at just the right moment tipped his hat to the crowd so the bird could fly away.

When Yankees general manager George Weiss campaigned to bring Stengel on board as skipper, Stengel had had years of experience managing—but all the teams he had managed in the majors had been losers. In fact, Stengel had only one winning season out of nine when he joined the Yankees in 1949. Casey was most famous as a clown, not as a winner. His coming to the Yankees was like a country bumpkin marrying a glamorous movie queen—the match seemed unlikely to last, let alone succeed.

"This is a big job, fellows," Stengel told reporters upon taking over the Yankees managing job, "and I barely have had time to study it. In fact, I scarcely know where I am at."

Casey Stengel playing a relaxed outfield for the Brooklyn Dodgers in 1915. (George Grantham Bain Collection, Library of Congress)

But those who scoffed at Casey overlooked something. He had learned his baseball by playing for such astute managers as John McGraw and Wilbert Robinson. He knew more about the game than most people ever learn. And he knew how to get the most from the players he worked with. Casey was an innovator in the use of his bench, employing a platoon system that was designed to get the most out of every man on his team. He was also an early proponent of the five-man starting pitching rotation. Once Casey took over in 1949, the Yankees went on to win the American League pennant in nine of the next ten years. From 1949 to 1953, the Yankees won an unmatched five World Series titles in a row, the most successful stretch in baseball history.

In 1950, with centerfielder Joe DiMaggio and shortstop Phil Rizzuto having great years at bat, and pitcher Vic Raschi's 21 wins second in the league, the Yankees again took first place, this time fighting off Detroit. As for the World Series, the Yankees swept the Philadelphia Phillies, known as the "Whiz Kids," in four straight games for their second consecutive world title. When asked about his theory of managing, Stengel said: "The secret of managing is to keep the five guys who hate you away from the five who are undecided."

Cleveland was the main threat to the Yankees in 1951, as fire-balling right-hander Bob Feller proved to be the best pitcher in the league and one of three pitchers to win 20 or more games for the Indians. The Yankees had two 21-game winners in Vic Raschi and Eddie Lopat. Allie Reynolds also pitched two no-hitters. But the team's hitting was very weak. Only one player—Gil McDougald, a rookie infielder—hit over .300. Yogi Berra, however, had 88 runs batted in to lead the team. The Yanks suffered a severe blow when DiMaggio was injured toward the close of the year. To replace him, Stengel daringly dipped into the Yankee farm system and called on a converted shortstop named Mickey Mantle. Overcoming all their shortcomings, the Yankees finished five games ahead of Cleveland. The World Series with the Giants went to six games, but the results were the same as in the previous two years—another Yankees triumph in the Fall Classic.

When DiMaggio retired prior to the 1952 season, Stengel reshaped the team around catcher Yogi Berra, pitcher Whitey Ford, and Stengel's special protégé, Mickey Mantle. As the season got underway, fans and sportswriters realized that Stengel and the Yankees had

Part Three

Mickey Mantle and Casey Stengel, 1956. (Courtesy of the Boston Public Library, Leslie Jones Collection)

a chance to equal a record by winning four World Series in a row, accomplished by Joe McCarthy's Yankees between 1936 and 1939. To take the pennant in 1952, the Yanks had to fight off Cleveland's powerful pitching staff of three 20-game winners—Early Wynn, Bob Lemon, and Mike Garcia. But the Yankees did win the pennant, even though Mantle and outfielder Gene Woodling were the only two players to hit over .300. The Yankees then triumphed over the Dodgers in the Series to tie the McCarthy-Yankees record of the 1930s. Now that they had tied the record, could Stengel's Yankees do what had never been done—capture the pennant and the World Series for the fifth time in a row?

The answer was a resounding yes.

The 1953 Yankees, stronger than the year before, won the pennant easily, finishing in front of Cleveland by 8½ games. Left-handed starting pitchers Whitey Ford and Eddie Lopat won 34 games between them. In the World Series against the Brooklyn Dodgers, Billy Martin, the Yankees' aggressive second baseman, dominated play. He hit two homers, two triples, a double and seven singles as the Yankees won the Series in six games. Mantle swung a potent bat, too, driving in seven runs with five hits, including a grand slam home run.

Billy Martin (right) and teammate Bobby Brown in Boston, 1951. In the 1953 World Series, he would lead the Yankees to a fifth consecutive world championship, the team's sixteenth title overall. (Courtesy of the Boston Public Library, Leslie Jones Collection.)

The Yankees threatened to make it six World Series wins in a row in 1954, but the Indians, still getting great pitching from Wynn, Lemon, and Garcia, beat them out. To do it, however, Cleveland had to win 111 games, a record for the American League. (The 1998 Yankees would better the mark with 114 wins.)

Over the next six years, the Yankees won five more American League titles. Their record of ten pennants and seven World Series victories in twelve years (1949-60) made them the dominant team of the 1950s and the most successful baseball dynasty in history.

Casey's Yankees would also win championships in 1956 and 1958. The unlikely marriage between Stengel and the Yanks turned out to be just about perfect. But it wasn't a perfect ending when the Yankees "retired" him following the 1960 World Series defeat, labeling him too old to manage. He was seventy. "I'll never make the mistake of being seventy again," he said.

The expansion New York Mets hired him as their first manager in 1962, and the 1962 Mets, with a 40-120 record, was the worst team in baseball history. Stengel served as front man for a team of lovable losers he dubbed "the Amazin' Metsies" for three more woeful seasons before retiring in 1965. The next year, Stengel was elected to the Hall of Fame, and his No. 37 jersey retired by both the Yankees and the Mets.

SPEAKIN' STENGELESE

Nicknamed "The Ol' Perfesser," Stengel was one of the most colorful characters in baseball history. He had a funny way of expressing himself, and the media dubbed his variation on English as "Stengelese."

Stengel died in 1975, but his Stengelese will live forever. In 1958, Stengel testified before a Senate subcommittee that was discussing a bill to officially recognize baseball's antitrust exemption, which bound a player to a team for life. When Stengel was asked why baseball wanted this bill passed, he replied in classic Stengelese:

"I would say I would not know, but I would say the reason they want it passed is to keep baseball going as the highest-paid ball sport that has gone into baseball, and from the baseball angle—I am not going to speak of any other sport. I am not here to argue about these other sports. I am in the baseball business. It has been run cleaner than any other business that was ever put out in the one hundred years at the present time."

Mickey Mantle testified next and was asked the same question. He smiled and replied: "My views are just about the same as Casey's."

1955

It's Déjà vu All Over Again

For pure staying power, no dynasty compares to the New York Yankees' version of 1949 to 1964. Those Yankees won nine World Series in fourteen tries over sixteen seasons, including a record five straight championships from 1949 to 1953. The constant of that era was their catcher, Yogi Berra. So integral was Berra to the Yankees' fortunes that he was voted the winner of the American League's most valuable player award three times (1951, 1954, and 1955) over a five-year span—in a league that boasted such future Hall of Fame stars as Mickey Mantle, Ted Williams, and Al Kaline. Even more impressive, from 1950 to 1957, Berra never finished lower than fourth in the MVP voting.

Bridging the team's transition from Joe DiMaggio to Mantle, Berra played on all fourteen pennant-winners during that prodigious stretch. He is the only player in history to play on ten World Series championship teams. He holds World Series records for at-bats (259), games (75), hits (71), and doubles (10). He played nineteen years in the majors and played in fifteen straight All-Star Games. When he retired, his 305 career home runs as a catcher (358 overall) stood as the record for catchers until Johnny Bench, Carlton Fisk, and then Mike Piazza broke it.

Lawrence Peter Berra grew up in an Italian section of St. Louis called "The Hill." He got his nickname as a kid after his friends saw an Indian actor in a movie that reminded them of Berra and from that point on, Larry was Yogi (a Hindu word for teacher). Berra began his career in the Yankees' farm system in 1943. He served in the Navy during World War II from 1944 to 1946, then joined the Yankees' top minor league team in Newark, New Jersey, where Mel Ott, the New York Giants manager, saw him play. "He seemed to be doing everything wrong, yet everything came out right," said Ott. "He stopped everything behind the plate and hit everything in front of it."

When Berra joined the Yankees in 1946 he was a backup player, sharing the catching duties and occasionally playing left field. In Yankee Stadium, left field is notorious for its late afternoon shadows. "It gets late early out there," he once said of the stadium.

Berra was squat and clumsy when he joined the Yankees. One writer said he looked like "the bottom man on an unemployed acrobatic team." Some teammates mocked him as "the Ape" by hanging from the dugout roof by one arm. But manager Casey Stengel believed in Berra from the start. Berra knew how to call a game, and Stengel dubbed him "my assistant manager." Yankees catcher Bill Dickey had just finished his Hall of Fame career, and he took the young Berra on as a student. Dickey was a great teacher, showing Berra the basics of catching, and Berra proved to be an excellent pupil.

In 1949, Berra became the Yankees full-time starting catcher, a job he would hold for ten years. Behind the plate Berra was one of the top defensive catchers in the game and a great handler of pitchers. The jug-eared catcher who was built like a fireplug had cat-like quickness. "He springs on a bunt like it was another dollar," said Stengel. Berra led the league in games caught eight times, led in double plays as a catcher six times and went the entire 1958 season without an error. He called two no-hitters thrown by Allie Reynolds in 1951 and caught Don Larsen's perfect game in the 1956 World Series—the only one in Series history. "It never happened before, and it still hasn't happened since," said Berra.

Playing for the Yankees, Berra had the opportunity to show his talents year after year in the World Series. Berra's great catching played a big part in the team's success, and so did his solid bat. He was one of the great clutch hitters of his day, "the toughest man in baseball in the last three innings," said Paul Richards, who managed the Orioles and White Sox during the 1950s. Berra was an amazing bad-ball hitter. Berra was skilled at reaching for balls out of the strike zone and hitting them out of the park. Yet for all his aggressiveness at the plate, he rarely struck out—only 414 times in 7,555 at-bats. In 1950 he fanned only twelve times in 597 at-bats. During that 1950 season, though not one of his MVP seasons, he hit a career-best .322 with 28 homers and 124 runs batted in. Berra drove in at least 90 runs nine times during his career.

By the late 1950s, with the emergence of Elston Howard at catcher, Berra had moved to left field to save his legs. From there, he helped the Yankees win two more World Series in 1961 and 1962. Just three weeks after playing in his final World Series game, in 1963, Berra was named the Yankees' manager, taking over a team that had just won four American League pennants in as many years. "If I can't manage, I'll quit," said Berra. "If I'm good, I'll stick around a little longer."

In 1964, with Berra at the helm, the Yankees won the pennant but lost the World Series to the St. Louis Cardinals in seven games. The day after the Series ended the Yankees fired Berra. The team finished sixth in 1965, and didn't appear in the World Series again until 1976 when Berra came back as a coach. In the meantime, the Mets hired Berra as a coach, reuniting him with Stengel. Berra remained with the Mets long after Stengel retired, and when manager Gil Hodges died unexpectedly in 1972, Berra took over as

Part Three

Yankee catchers Yogi Berra (left) and Elston Howard in 1955. (Courtesy of the Boston Public Library, Leslie Jones Collection.)

skipper. In 1973 he managed the Mets to their second National League pennant and became only the second manager in major league history to win pennants in both leagues. (The first was Joe McCarthy.) Those "Ya Gotta Believe" Mets came from last place in the final month of the season to win the NLeastern division with the lowest winning percentage of any division winner in history. This was the year when Berra coined the memorable phrase, "It ain't over 'til it's over."

Berra returned to the Yankees as a coach in 1976 and then as a manager again in 1984 and part of 1985. George Steinbrenner fired him sixteen games into the 1985 season. Steinbrenner had promised before the season that Berra would be the manager for the entire '85 season, "no matter what." But when the White Sox swept a three-game series from the Bombers, Steinbrenner fired Berra and hired Billy Martin for a fourth time. Berra was so hurt that he stayed away from Yankee Stadium for fifteen years. The two men made up during the winter of 1998, and Berra returned to the Bronx to throw out the first pitch on opening day in 1999. Later that summer, on Yogi Berra Day, David Cone pitched a perfect game as Berra and Don Larsen looked on. Until his death in September 2015, Berra spent most of his time working at the Yogi Berra Museum in New Jersey. He was elected to baseball's Hall of Fame in 1972 and was chosen to baseball's All-Century Team for the 1900s.

YOGI-ISMS

Yogi Berra is known to many people as the inventor of "Yogi-isms," Berra's own brand of rearranging the English language and warping logic. It's ironic that the master of Yogi-isms was managed for most of his Yankees career by baseball's other great reinventor of the English language, the originator of "Stengelese," Casey Stengel. Here is a list of some of Berra's most famous Yogi-isms:

- "If you can't imitate him, don't copy him."
- "I knew I was going to take the wrong train, so I left early."
- "I want to thank you for making this day necessary."
- "Baseball is 90 percent mental. The other half is physical."
- "You can observe a lot by watching."
- "A nickel ain't worth a dime anymore."
- "If the world were perfect, it wouldn't be."
- "It's déjà vu all over again."
- "Nobody goes to that restaurant anymore; it's too crowded."
- "Slump? I ain't in no slump; I just ain't hitting."
- "I made a wrong mistake."
- "If you come to a fork in the road … take it."
- "In baseball, you don't know nothing."
- "You should always go to other people's funerals; otherwise, they won't come to yours."
- "It ain't the heat; it's the humility."
- "If the fans don't come out to the ball park, you can't stop them."
- "I always thought that record would stand until it was broken."
- "I really didn't say everything I said."

1956

The Mick's Triple Crown

Few players in the history of baseball had as much talent as Mickey Mantle. The blond, broad-shouldered switch hitter from Commerce, Oklahoma, could blast the ball for tremendous distances from either side of the plate. He also had a fine throwing arm and great speed—he could run from home to first base in 3.1 seconds. Mantle's natural talent once prompted his manager, Casey Stengel, to say of the slugging center fielder: "He should lead the league in everything."

In 1956, he did. That season, Mantle won the most valuable player award and became the only switch-hitter to win the batting Triple Crown—leading the league in batting average, home runs, and runs batted in. He hit .353 to Ted Williams' .345 for the Red Sox; his 52 homers were far ahead of Vic Wertz's 32 for the Indians; and his 130 runs batted in topped Al Kaline's 128 for the Tigers. He also led the league in runs scored (132), total bases (376), slugging percentage (.705), extra base hits (79) and most times reaching base safely (302). Then he capped off his great season with three homers in the 1956 World Series, won by the Yankees over the Brooklyn Dodgers in seven games. Mantle was just twenty-four years old. He continued his offensive prowess in 1957 and repeated as the league's most valuable player, batting a career-high .365, with 34 homers and 94 RBI.

"The Mick" played his first major league game when he was nineteen years old. He played for eighteen seasons beginning in 1951, when he was a rookie for the Yankees' World Series champs. He suffered a serious knee injury in the outfield during Game 2 of the series against the New York Giants that year. The injury robbed him of much of his speed and troubled him throughout the rest of his career. As teammate Jerry Coleman said, The Mick had "the body of a god. Only Mantle's legs were mortal." Still, he managed to belt 536 career home runs—the most ever by a switch-hitter.

Despite an injury-riddled career, Mantle put up impressive numbers. He played in twenty All-Star Games, led the league in home runs four times and hit .300 or better ten times. He was a three-time American League most valuable player and finished in the top five another six times. He played on twelve pennant winners and seven world championship teams. He holds World Series record for home runs (18), runs scored (42), RBI (40), walks (43), extra-base hits (26), and total bases (123). "He is the best one-legged player I ever saw play the game," said Stengel.

In his final World Series, in 1964 against the St. Louis Cardinals, Mantle hit three round trippers, drove in eight runs, and batted .333. That season marked the end of the lengthy Yankees dynasty that had started in the 1920s with Babe Ruth, and peaked in the years from 1949 to 1964. Mantle's fortunes sank along with those of his team. By 1968 he could no longer take the pain of playing every day and his numbers reflected it. At thirty-seven, he had undergone seven surgeries in his career. On the eve of the 1969 season, Mantle decided that he did not want to sign a contract, and he retired.

The team and fans paid tribute to this great superstar of the Yankees dynasty by retiring his uniform jersey No. 7 at a Mickey Mantle Day ceremony at Yankee Stadium, on June 8, 1969. In his speech, Mantle spoke of the Yankees' tradition. "To retire my number with numbers 3, 4, and 5 tops off everything," he said. "I often wondered how a man who knew he was dying could get up here and say he's the luckiest man in the world. Now I think I know how Lou Gehrig felt."

Mantle was elected to the Hall of Fame in 1974. As the first baseball star Yankee fans could watch on television, he remains a fan favorite and is still one of baseball's most popular superstars even forty-five years after playing his last game. Early in 1995 he was diagnosed with liver cancer, brought on by his years of hard drinking. He had a liver transplant but died in August of that year at age sixty-three.

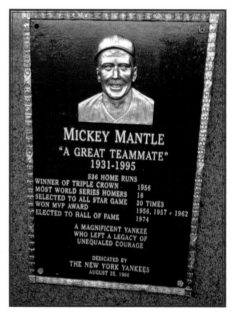

Mickey Mantle's plaque in Yankee Stadium's Monument Park. (Acruz318 via Wikimedia Commons)

MVP! MVP! MVP!

Yankees players have won the American League's most valuable player award 22 times since the award was instituted in 1911. That's the most winning players of any team in major league baseball. (The St. Louis Cardinals are second most with 17 players winning the National League award.)

By the rules of the American League at the time, Babe Ruth was ineligible for the MVP award in his famous (and deserving) 1927 season because he had previously won in 1923.

Elston Howard, the first African American player in Yankees history, was the 1963 American League's most valuable player—the first African American to win the award in the AL. (African American players had won it in the National League 11 times.) Howard hit .287 with 28 home runs and 85 runs batted in to lead New York to the A.L. pennant. A two-time Gold Glove catcher, Howard played over 1,400 games with the Yankees and was a member of AL pennant-winning Yankees teams in nine of his first ten seasons. A respected clubhouse leader, Howard retired in 1968 and became a Yankees coach until his death in 1980.

Alex Rodriguez is the only player in baseball history to win the Most Valuable Player award with two different teams and at two different positions. He won the award as a shortstop for the Texas Rangers in 2003 and as a third baseman with the Yankees in 2005 and 2007.

Yankees' Most Valuable Player Award Winners		
Year	Player	Position
1923	Babe Ruth	Outfield
1927	Lou Gehrig	First base
1936	Lou Gehrig	First base
1939	Joe DiMaggio	Outfield
1941	Joe DiMaggio	Outfield
1942	Joe Gordon	Second base
1943	Spud Chandler	Pitcher
1947	Joe DiMaggio	Outfield
1950	Phil Rizzuto	Shortstop
1951	Yogi Berra	Catcher
1954	Yogi Berra	Catcher
1955	Yogi Berra	Catcher
1956	Mickey Mantle	Outfield
1957	Mickey Mantle	Outfield

Year	Player	Position
1960	Roger Maris	Outfield
1961	Roger Maris	Outfield
1962	Mickey Mantle	Outfield
1963	Elston Howard	Catcher
1976	Thurman Munson	Catcher
1985	Don Mattingly	First base
2005	Alex Rodriguez	Third base
2007	Alex Rodriguez	Third base

Part Three

1956

World Series Perfection

Not every great pitching accomplishment in baseball is the work of a superstar like Whitey Ford or Roger Clemens who enjoyed a long and stellar career. In fact, the most remarkable pitching feat in baseball history was achieved by Don Larsen, a journeyman who is remembered for what he did in a single game. The classic pitching performance occurred in the 1956 World Series between the New York Yankees and the Brooklyn Dodgers.

In Larsen's first World Series appearance, in 1955, the Dodgers beat him up, scoring five times in his four innings of work. In 1956, the twenty-six-year-old right-hander had a good season, going 11-5 despite battling control issues. Starting Game 2 of the Series, he was staked to a 6-0 lead after an inning and a half. But after an infield error and a couple of walks, he was gone. The Yankees relievers didn't stem the tide and Larsen's log after an inning and two-thirds was four runs allowed. Brooklyn won 13-8.

Yankees manager Casey Stengel later admitted his second-inning hook of Larsen might have been too quick. "However," said Stengel, "it might also help to get him really on his toes the next time he starts."

Three days later, Larsen had pinpoint control, going to three balls on just one hitter. In the early innings, he retired three hitters in a row every inning. Few Dodgers even came close to reaching base. By the middle of the ball game, the Yankee Stadium crowd of 64,519 fans woke up to the fact that Larsen was pitching a perfect game. The tension kept mounting as the game rolled on.

"In the seventh inning I noticed no one on the bench was talking to me," said Larsen.

The tension reached its peak in the ninth inning. Carl Furillo was the first hitter Larsen faced. He was out on an easy fly ball. Roy Campanella, the next hitter, grounded out. The crowd hushed as it was now obvious that all that stood between Larsen and a history-making game was the pinch-hitter, a left-handed batter named Dale Mitchell.

"Ball one!" was the call on the first pitch.

Larsen rocked forward on the mound. His arm flashed downward.

"Stee-rike!"

Larsen kicked and fired again. Mitchell lashed at the ball and missed. It was strike two. Mitchell swung at the next pitch. This time he connected. The ball went foul.

The umpire threw a new ball into play. Larsen rubbed the slickness from the cover. He glanced about the diamond, took a deep breath, and stepped on the rubber.

Then Larsen's 97th pitch, a fastball on the outside corner, was called strike three by umpire Babe Pinelli, sending catcher Yogi Berra jumping into Larsen's arms to celebrate the only perfect game in World Series history.

Part Three

Yogi Berra leaps into Don Larsen's arms after the final out of Larsen's perfect game in the 1956 World Series. (AP Photo, File)

"It never happened before, and it still hasn't happened since," said Berra.

Of course, Larsen had plenty of support, including a one-handed running catch by the fleet Mickey Mantle in center. A hard liner by Jackie Robinson off the hands of third baseman Andy Carey was alertly snapped up by shortstop Gil McDougald and turned into an out. Larsen also struck out seven batters in the 2-0 victory.

The Yankees went on to win the Series in seven games, thanks to a journeyman pitcher who had triumphed at a time when the Yankees needed it most with one of the most spectacular achievements in baseball history. Indeed, the Series will forever belong to an imperfect man who pitched a perfect game.

"It can't be true," he said after the game. "Any minute now I expect the alarm clock to ring and someone to say, 'Okay, Larsen, it's time to get up.'"

Larsen, who finished his career with an 81-91 record, was an unlikely candidate to make history. Following the perfecto, his career lasted eleven more seasons with six different teams. He never again approached the glory of October 8, 1956. But who could?

1957

Incident at the Copa

Whenever he put on the Yankees uniform as a player or as a manager, Billy Martin instilled a fiery emotion in his teams. Unfortunately, he is best remembered as a hard-drinking brawler whose battles during the 1970s with Reggie Jackson and George Steinbrenner turned Yankee Stadium into the Bronx Zoo.

Martin's passion for drinking and fighting overshadowed a brilliant career as a clutch performer. His lifetime batting average of .333 in five World Series is one of the best for players with at least 75 series at bats. He made a terrific running catch in 1952 to save Game 7 for the Yankees. The following year he hit .500 to lead the Bombers to their fifth straight title. As a manager, his burning desire to win helped propel the Yankees to the American League pennant in 1976 and a World Series championship in 1977.

Martin's defining on-field moment came during Game 7 of the 1952 World Series against the Brooklyn Dodgers at Ebbets Field. With the Yankees holding a tenuous 4-2 lead in the seventh inning, the Dodgers had the bases loaded with two outs and Jackie Robinson at bat. That's when the scrappy second baseman made the play of the series. Robinson hit a seemingly innocent little popup on the infield, but first baseman Joe Collins looked up and lost the ball in the sun. Pitcher Bob Kuzava stood transfixed on the mound. Third baseman Gil McDougald was too far away to catch it. Martin, the second baseman, realized that no one was going for the ball. It looked as if the ball might fall safely to the ground—with disastrous results for the Yankees. But Billy Martin came to the rescue for New York. He darted in and made a game-saving knee-high catch between the pitcher's mound and first base. Their rally snuffed out, that was it for the Dodgers. Kuzava got out of the inning and got Brooklyn out in the eighth and ninth to save it. The Yankees were champions of baseball for the fourth consecutive season.

In 1953, for the second year in a row, Martin was one of the heroes as the Yankees again defeated the Dodgers in the series, this time in six games. Martin hit a single in the bottom of the ninth inning of game six, breaking a 3-3 tie and driving in the series-clinching run. The winning hit capped a brilliant series for Martin. He batted .500 with 12 hits, two homers, two triples, and a team-leading eight runs batted in.

Martin's defining off-field moment prompted the Yankees to send him packing. Martin and six teammates were involved in a late-night brawl with members of a bowling team during a Sammy Davis Jr. show at the Copacabana nightclub, in Manhattan, on May 16, 1957. (The Copa, then at 10 East 60th Street, is now located in Times Square at 268 W. 47th Street.) Martin along with teammates Mickey Mantle, Whitey Ford, Yogi Berra, Gil McDougald, Johnny Kucks, and Hank Bauer, were at the club to celebrate Billy's twenty-ninth birthday when the altercation occurred. A reputation for post-midnight alcohol-fueled donnybrooks had followed Martin around since 1952, so it came as no surprise, despite manager Casey Stengel's affection for Martin, when the Yankees held him responsible for the incident. Four weeks later, Martin was traded to the Kansas City Athletics in a deal generally acknowledged to have stemmed from the brawl.

Martin's playing career ended in 1961 and after brief and turbulent stints in the manager's office in Minnesota, Detroit, and Texas, the combative former Yankee was hired by new owner George Steinbrenner. Martin's tenure in the Bronx under Steinbrenner began on a high note, with the Yankees winning the American League pennant in 1976 and the World Series in 1977. That season, two and a half months into his Yankee playing tenure, Reggie Jackson was already in Martin's doghouse. In the sixth inning of a nationally televised game between the Yankees and the Boston Red Sox at Fenway Park, on June 18, 1977, Martin thought Jackson had been loafing when he failed to hustle on a Jim Rice blooper that landed for a double. When Martin made a pitching change, he also sent Paul Blair to right field to replace Reggie. Jackson was understandably not happy when he returned to the dugout. The manager and slugger exchanged heated words in the dugout and were separated by coaches Elston Howard and Yogi Berra before any punches landed. The incident was broadcast on national television.

The Martin versus Jackson feud came to a head in July 1978, when Reggie bunted despite Martin's order to swing away. Martin suspended Jackson for five games for insubordination, but Steinbrenner ordered his star slugger reinstated, prompting Martin to fire back with his notorious quip: "The two of them deserve each other. One's a born liar, the other's convicted." Martin quit the next day. He would eventually be re-hired four more times.

During his five separate stints as New York's skipper, Martin became involved in several highly publicized drunken fights that each time would lead to his undoing. "Billy the Kid" got bounced from a Texas strip club; threw punches at pitcher Ed Whitson in the parking lot of a Baltimore drinking establishment; and flattened a marshmallow salesman at a hotel bar in Minnesota, to name but a few incidents.

"Lots of people look up to Billy Martin," said former Yankees pitcher Jim Bouton. "That's because he just knocked them down."

Alcohol also played a part in Martin's death on a snowy Christmas Day in 1989. The sixty-one-year-old was a passenger in a car driven by his friend when the vehicle slid off the road and crashed in upstate New York, less than a mile from Martin's home. Both men were drunk at the time of the accident. The driver survived, but Billy did not.

HIRED TO BE FIRED

New York Yankees owner George Steinbrennner made twenty-one managerial changes between 1973 and 2007, including the hiring of firing of Billy Martin five times. The Martin-Steinbrenner relationship bordered on comical, with Martin being fired four times as the Yankees manager (he resigned once). Here is the Steinbrenner Managerial Merry Go Round.

September 30, 1973	Ralph Houk resigned.
January 3, 1974	Bill Virdon hired.
August 1, 1975	Virdon fired. Billy Martin hired.
July 24, 1978	Martin resigned.
July 25, 1978	Bob Lemon hired.
July 29, 1978	Martin hired for 1980.
June 18, 1979	Lemon fired. Martin hired.
October 28, 1979	Martin fired. Dick Howser hired.
November 21, 1980	Howser's resignation announced. Gene Michael hired.
September 6, 1981	Michael fired. Lemon hired.
April 26, 1982	Lemon fired. Michael hired.
August 3, 1982	Michael fired. Clyde King hired as interim manager.
January 11, 1983	Martin hired.
December 16, 1983	Martin fired. Yogi Berra hired.
April 28, 1985	Berra fired. Martin hired.
October 27, 1985	Martin fired. Lou Piniella hired.
October 19, 1987	Piniella promoted. Martin hired.
June 23, 1988	Martin fired. Piniella hired.
October 7, 1988	Piniella fired. Dallas Green hired.
August 18, 1989	Green fired. Bucky Dent hired.
June 6, 1990	Dent fired. Stump Merrill hired.
October 7, 1991	Stump Merrill fired.
October 29, 1991	Buck Showalter hired.
October 26, 1995	Showalter's resignation announced.
November 2, 1995	Joe Torre hired.
Oct. 18, 2007	Torre rejects new contract offer.
Oct. 30, 2007	Joe Girardi hired.

Part Three

1960

Mazeroski Slays Goliath

Bobby Richardson of the Yankees is the only player from the losing team to win the World Series most valuable player award. In the 1960 World Series won by the Pittsburgh Pirates in seven games, Richardson drove in a Series-record six runs in Game 3 on his way to a record 12 runs batted in for the Series. The Yankees' second baseman, having driven in just 26 runs for the season, flexed his muscles in this Series. He had 11 hits, including two triples, two doubles, a grand slam home run, and eight runs scored. His record of six RBI in a World Series game stood alone in the record book for forty-nine years until another Yankees World Series most valuable player, Hideki Matsui, equaled the feat in the clinching Game 6 of the 2009 World Series.

Looking at the statistics, the 1960 World Series should have been won by the New York Yankees. The Bronx Bombers set a number of Series records—highest batting average (.338), most hits (91), most runs (55), and most runs batted in (54). But this October, the Yankees lost to the Pittsburgh Pirates, four games to three, on one of the most dramatic endings to a Game 7 in World Series history.

The first six games of the 1960 Series had taken on an unusual tone with the Pirates winning three games by close scores and the Yankees winning three games by a combined 35 runs. After the Pirates won the opener, 6-4, the Yankees came back in Games 2 and 3 with a vengeance to pound the Pirates to a pulp, 16-3, and 10-0. Mickey Mantle homered twice in Game 2 and Bobby Richardson drove in a Series-record six runs in Game 3 on his way to a record 12 RBI for the Series.

Pittsburgh tamed New York's bats in winning Games 4 and 5 by scores of 3-2 and 5-2. New York answered in Game 6 by routing the Pirates, 12-0, behind Whitey Ford's second shutout of the Series. In the deciding seventh game, New York rolled to a 7-4 lead in the eighth inning. Just six outs separated the Yankees from their 19th title. "I thought that would do it," said Yogi Berra. "We had a lot of good pitchers to hold the lead."

But the Pirates stormed back in the bottom of the eighth inning, scoring five runs to take a 9-7 advantage. The key play was a ground ball to Tony Kubek that took a bad hop and hit the Yankee shortstop in the throat, allowing the Pittsburgh rally to continue. In the top of the ninth inning, with the Yankees on the verge of defeat, Mantle singled to score one run, and then made a sensational base-running play to elude a tag, allowing the tying run to score.

That set the stage for Pittsburgh second baseman Bill Mazeroski, the leadoff batter in the bottom of the ninth. Ralph Terry, the fifth Yankee pitcher in the game, threw one ball and, on the second pitch, Mazeroski swung and blasted a high fly ball that cleared the left-field wall for a home run to win the Series for the Pirates. Mazeroski jumped up and down, waving his cap in the air, going wild around the bases. There were so many people on the field blocking his way by the time he rounded third base, he barely made it around to touch home plate. He did make it home, though, and the Pirates won, 10-9. The home run brought a dramatic conclusion to an improbable Series in which the resourceful Pirates had been out hit, 91-60, and outscored, 55-27.

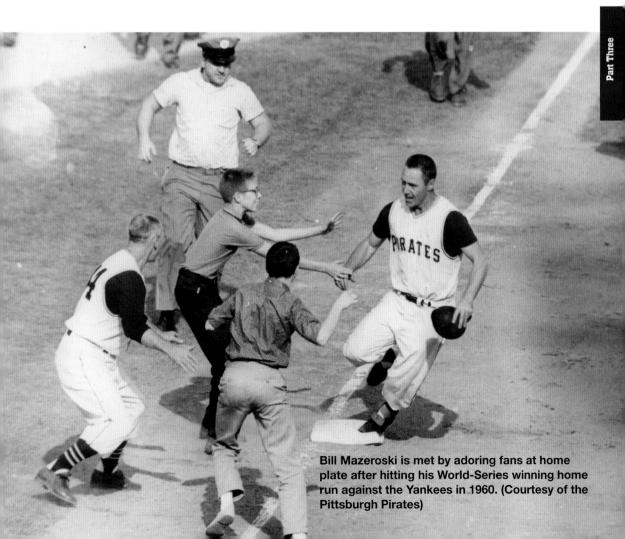

Bill Mazeroski is met by adoring fans at home plate after hitting his World-Series winning home run against the Yankees in 1960. (Courtesy of the Pittsburgh Pirates)

Part Three

1961

61 in '61

In 1961, the New York Yankees won 109 games and fueled by Mickey Mantle and Roger Maris—the "M & M Boys"—hit an earth-shaking 240 home runs, a record that stood for thirty-four years. The team's top sluggers were Maris with a record 61, Mantle with 54, Bill Skowron with 28, Yogi Berra with 22, Elston Howard with 21, and back-up catcher and pinch-hitter Johnny Blanchard with 21.

Sluggers Roger Maris (left) and Mickey Mantle had a combined season for the ages in 1961. (Courtesy of the Boston Public Library, Leslie Jones Collection)

That year, Maris and Mantle both made a run at Ruth's single-season home run record of 60, established in 1927. At the time this was the most famous record in baseball. Mantle started out red-hot, but injuries forced him to drop out of the race in mid-September with 54 homers. Maris continued his march toward the Babe's season record. Maris had a compact, left-handed swing that was perfect for the short right-field porch at Yankee Stadium. As it became apparent that the twenty-seven-year-old Maris would challenge Ruth's record, baseball commissioner Ford C. Frick announced that since Ruth's record was set in a 154-game season—and the Yankees in the expansion era of 1961 were playing 162 games—Maris would not be recognized as the one-season home run champion if he hit his 61st homer after the 154-game mark. A home-run record accomplished after the team's 155th game, according to Frick's infamous ruling, would receive second billing to Ruth.

As Maris reached 50 home runs, it looked as though Ruth's record *might* be broken within the 154-game period. By game 130, Maris had 51 homers. At that same point, Ruth had belted out 49. With 57 homers, Maris was one ahead of Ruth's pace for 150 games. In game 152, he hit his 58th homer. Maris conceded the odds were against him, and the pressure of making a run at one of baseball's most cherished records was so intense that it made his hair fall out in clumps.

Maris hit home run number 59 during the 155th game. According to Frick's ruling, Ruth's record still stood. Four games later Maris hit number 60. And on the final day of the season, the Yankees were playing the Boston Red Sox in Yankee Stadium. There wasn't even a sellout at the Stadium, with only 23,154 fans in attendance. In the fourth inning, on a two balls and no strikes count, Maris connected with a Tracey Stallard fastball and sent it flying over the right-field wall. The new home run king rounded the bases with stoic grace, got a handshake from third-base coach Frank Crosetti, and was convinced by teammates in the dugout to make a reluctant curtain call. "I knew it was gone the minute I hit it," Maris said. "I can't explain how I felt. I don't know what I was thinking as I rounded the bases. My mind was blank."

Maris's 61st home run in '61 was one more than Ruth hit in 1927—though the milestone homer didn't erase Ruth's record. Frick, true to his word, had Maris's accomplishment listed after Ruth's feat in the record books, in effect telling Maris that he was second fiddle to Ruth. No asterisk in the baseball record book noting that Roger Maris set his single-season home run record in 163 games (statistics from one postponed game also counted in 1961) while Babe Ruth reached his in 154 really ever existed—the records were simply listed separately. But the twin listing itself ignited a controversy, implying to some that Maris's record was somehow inferior. The humble man from Fargo, North Dakota, was no folk hero like Ruth, but he deserved credit for his amazing performance. "As a ballplayer, I would be delighted to do it again," he said. "As an individual, I doubt if I could possibly go through it again."

In all, Maris hit 275 homers in a twelve-season career from 1957 to 1968. In 1961, he led the American League in runs (132), runs batted in (141), and of course home runs

(61), and was the American League's most valuable player for a second straight season, a testament to his all-around ability.

"Roger Maris was the best all-around baseball player I ever saw," said Mantle. "Roger was a great fielder, he had a great arm, he was a great base runner, he was always mentally in the game, and he never made a mistake throwing too high or to the wrong base. Roger was as good as there ever was."

Maris hit 33 homers the year after his record-breaking season, and though he never topped 26 again, he was a winner. No one in the 1960s appeared in more World Series than Maris, who played in seven that decade. Five came with the Yankees, the last two in 1967 and '68 came with the Cardinals.

No matter how it was cataloged in the record book, fans always recognized Maris as the true record-holder, the first player in major league history to hit more than 60 homers in a regular season. In 1991, baseball commissioner Fay Vincent made it official, announcing that a major-league baseball committee on statistical accuracy had voted to remove the distinction, giving the record fully to Maris. Sadly, he did not live to see the change, having died of cancer in Houston at age fifty-one in 1985.

Maris held the single-season home run record for thirty-seven years—longer than Ruth had held it—until the steroid era when Mark McGwire of the St. Louis Cardinals surpassed the mark with 70 homers in 1998. His record was subsequently broken when the San Francisco Giants' Barry Bonds hit 73 home runs in the 2001 season.

LIGHTING UP THE SCOREBOARD

The Yankees hit a franchise record 245 home runs in 2012, surpassing the mark first set by the 1961 team and later bested by the 2004 and 2009 teams. But a scoring record set by the 1932 Bronx Bombers can never be broken. That season, the Yankees scored at least one run in every game played, becoming the only team in major league history not shut out over an entire season. They were held to one run in 11 games, and won three of those. The Yankees led baseball with 1,002 runs scored and 107 wins in 1932. Incredibly, their only players to lead the American League in a major offensive category was Ben Chapman with 38 stolen bases and Babe Ruth with a .489 on-base percentage.

The Bombers scored at least one run in 308 straight games from August 3, 1931, to August 2, 1933—the big league record for consecutive games without being shut out. The Yankees were not silenced in the final 55 games of the 1931 season after August 1 and did not get blanked again until August 3, 1933, when their streak ended at 308 games. The streak was broken by a 1-0 shutout pitched by the future Hall of Fame left-hander, Lefty Grove, of the Philadelphia Athletics.

1961

Ford Keeps Rolling

Edward Charles "Whitey" Ford was the ace of the New York Yankees pitching staff in the 1950s and early '60s. The only Yankees pitcher of that era to make it into the Hall of Fame, Ford is the club's all-time leader in wins, games started, innings pitched, and shutouts.

Ford's lifetime record of 236-106 gives him a career winning percentage of .690, the highest among any major league pitcher since 1900 with 200 or more wins. Ford changed his pitch speeds expertly, mixing up a solid fastball, a sharp breaking curve, and a very effective change-up. A top-notch fielder, he also had one of the league's great pick-off

Part Three

Whitey Ford pitching against the Orioles in 1961. (AP Photo)

moves. All this resulted in a consistently low earned run average that stayed below 3.00 in eleven of his sixteen major league seasons, never rising higher than 3.24 throughout his career. Ford led the American League in victories three times and in earned run average and shutouts twice. He won the Cy Young Award in 1961, when pitchers in both leagues competed for only one award.

Ford saved his most impressive performances for when it counted most—in the World Series. The Yankees won eleven pennants during Ford's years with the club, and he helped the Yankees win six World Series titles. "You kind of took it for granted around the Yankees that there was always going to be baseball in October," said Ford.

The lefthander still holds several important World Series pitching records, including most Series (11), most games started (22), most opening-game starts (8), most innings pitched (146), most strikeouts (94), and most wins (10). He allowed only 44 earned runs in his 22 World Series starts. "If the World Series was on the line and I could pick one pitcher to pitch the game, I'd choose Whitey Ford every time," said teammate and lifelong pal Mickey Mantle.

In 1960 and 1961, Ford started four World Series games, won them all, and allowed no runs. On his way to his fourth straight World Series shutout in Game Four of the 1961 Series, Ford injured his ankle and had to leave the game. He departed that game with a streak of 32 consecutive scoreless innings, having broken Babe Ruth's World Series record. As a Boston Red Sox pitcher, the Babe pitched 29 2/3 consecutive scoreless innings in the 1916 and 1918 World Series. Ruth would often say this was his proudest accomplishment in baseball, greater than any of his batting feats. In the 1962 Series, Ford continued his streak, ending up with 33 2/3 consecutive scoreless innings—still the World Series record.

Paul Krichell was a Yankees scout for thirty-seven years, and it was Krichell who first spotted and signed Ford (as well as Lou Gehrig and Phil Rizzuto in previous years). Krichell discovered the seventeen-year old first baseman in Astoria, Queens, not far from Yankee Stadium. Ford was only 5'9" and 150 pounds in high school and was too small to be a position player in the majors. So he switched to pitching full time. Ford made the Yankees' squad midway through the 1950 season, and he won his first nine games on his way to a 9-1 rookie record, helping the Yankees win the American League pennant his first season. That year, in his first of many World Series, Ford pitched eight and two-thirds innings without allowing an earned run, winning Game 4 of a four-game Yankees sweep over the Philadelphia Phillies.

Ford spent 1951 and 1952 in military service. He returned in 1953 and went 18-6, followed by a 16-8 record in 1954. His 18-7 record in 1955 tied him for most wins in the American League. He led the league with eighteen complete games, and finished second in earned run average (2.63), earning his first of eight All-Star selections. The next season he went 19-6, leading the A.L. in win percentage (.760) and earned run average (2.47). He also won the ERA title in 1958, with a 2.01 mark.

The Yankees' manager, Casey Stengel, limited Ford's starts, choosing to rest him four or five days between appearances, and thus saving him for use against the better teams in the league. Stengel would hold out Ford against cellar-dwelling teams like the Washington Senators and Philadelphia Athletics, so he could start against division rivals such as the Cleveland Indians and Detroit Tigers. Only once during the decade under Stengel did Ford start more than 30 games in a season. But in 1961, when Ralph Houk took over as the Yankees manager, he moved Ford into a regular four-man rotation and the durable lefty thrived on the bigger workload. In 1961, Ford led the league with 39 games started—ten more than the year before—and innings pitched (283). He posted a spectacular 25-4 record to lead the major leagues in wins and winning percentage (.862). That season, he won his only Cy Young Award and then earned the World Series Most Valuable Player Award. Two years later, at the age of thirty-five, he started 37 times and went 24-7. It's possible that Stengel's conservative use of Ford might have robbed the pitcher of at least 40 more career wins.

In 1963, Ford, who was known as "The Chairman of the Board," again led the league in wins (24), winning percentage (.774), games started (37), and innings pitched (269.1). The World Series that season between the Yankees and the Los Angeles Dodgers provided a showcase for the game's top two left-handed pitchers. Ford was the premier lefty in the American League. The Dodgers' Sandy Koufax had posted a 25-5 record and was the best lefty in the National League. The pitchers met in Game One. In the first inning Ford struck out two Dodgers and got the third out on an easy ground ball. Koufax struck out the first five Yankees batters and out-pitched Ford all afternoon. The Dodgers won 5-2, as Koufax struck out fifteen Yankees to set a Series record. Ford and Koufax met again in Game 4. This time Ford gave up just two hits in seven innings, but an error by Yankees first baseman Joe Pepitone proved costly and the Dodgers won the game, 2-1, to complete a Series sweep.

After thirteen straight seasons of at least 11 victories, Ford suffered his first losing seasons in 1966 and '67, his final major league campaigns. Still, he sported impressive earned run averages of 2.47 and 1.64, respectively. After retiring following the 1967 season, Whitey and his good buddy Mickey were enshrined in the Hall of Fame together in 1974.

Following his playing career, Ford admitted to throwing illegal pitches, primarily by having his catcher Elston Howard scuff the baseballs with mud before throwing the ball back to him on the mound. Ford also used a wedding ring with a sharp edge to nick the ball, causing the ball to sink more than his usual pitches. "I didn't begin cheating until late in my career, when I needed it to survive," Ford admitted. "I didn't cheat when I won the 25 games in 1961. I don't want anyone to get any ideas and take my Cy Young Award away. And I didn't cheat in 1963 when I won 24 games," he said, and then added with a sly smile, "well, maybe just a little."

1962

Terry's Redemption

Ralph Terry's name is synonymous with one of the most famous home runs in baseball history. In the 1960 World Series, the Yankees and Pittsburgh Pirates were deadlocked at three games apiece and the score was tied 9-9 in the deciding seventh game. Pittsburgh second baseman Bill Mazeroski was the leadoff batter in the bottom of the ninth inning against Terry. The right-hander threw one ball and, on Terry's second pitch, Mazeroski swung and blasted a high fly ball that cleared the Forbes Field left-field wall for a home run to win the Series for the Pirates. The home run was the most dramatic conclusion to a Game 7 in World Series history.

Afterward in the Yankee clubhouse, the press hounded Terry, the losing pitcher. When asked if he had thrown Mazeroski a fastball or curve, a dejected Terry said, "I don't know what the pitch was. All I know is it was the wrong one."

Two years later, Ralph Terry was standing nervously on the mound at San Francisco's Candlestick Park in the bottom of the 9th inning of Game 7 of the 1962 World Series. The Yankees were clinging to a 1-0 lead, but Matty Alou stood on third base as the tying run for the Giants, and Willie Mays was on second representing the winning run. The imposing figure coming up to bat was the left-handed slugging Willie McCovey, who had already blasted a tape-measure home run off Terry in Game 2 of the Series, and in his previous at-bat had hit a booming triple over the centerfielder's head.

Yankees manager Ralph Houk went to the mound to speak to his pitching ace. Terry was the American League's most winning and most durable pitcher in 1962 with 23 wins and 299 innings pitched. He also surrendered a league-high 40 home runs, the most ever given up by a Yankee pitcher in a season. Traditional strategy in such a tight spot says to intentionally walk McCovey, creating a force at any base, and pitching to the next batter, the right-handed hitting Orlando Cepeda, also no slouch. Houk asked his pitcher what he wanted to do.

"I'd just as soon get it over now," Terry replied.

At this tense moment Terry could only be thinking that he had been in this situation before. Two years earlier, Pittsburgh's Bill Mazeroski had led off the bottom of the ninth inning in Game 7 and hit a dramatic Series-winning home run off Terry. Now Terry was facing another confrontation that would end with him being a Series hero or goat. In baseball, the difference often is measured in inches.

Terry anxiously made his crucial decision to pitch to the 6-foot-4, 225-pound McCovey. If Terry could get McCovey out, it would be his Fall Classic redemption. With two outs and the World Series on the line, Terry let fly a fastball. McCovey nailed it, smashing a blistering line drive that was heading toward right field like a bullet. But Yankees second baseman Bobby Richardson speared the ball in his mitt for the final out.

New York Yankee starting pitchers left to right, Whitey Ford, Jim Bouton, Al Downing, Ralph Terry, and Stan Williams, September 4, 1963. (AP Photo)

"I really didn't have time to think about it," Richardson recalled. "It was just hit too hard."

The Yankees were champions for the second straight season and had captured the World Series flag for the twentieth time in their history. Terry, who was named the series Most Valuable Player, had atoned for losing the seventh game against Pittsburgh in 1960 by shutting out the Giants on four hits in a nerve-wracking Game 7 that clinched the 1962 Series for New York, four games to three.

McCovey's near-Series-winning hit was immortalized by *Peanuts* cartoonist and anguished Giants fan Charles M. Schulz, in a strip in which a glum Charlie Brown laments: "Why couldn't McCovey have hit the ball just three feet higher?"

1964

End of the Dynasty

Both the New York Yankees and St. Louis Cardinals made it to the 1964 World Series after heart-pounding pennant races. The Yankees, now skippered by Yogi Berra, rallied in September with an 11-game win streak to clinch the American League pennant on the next to last day of the season. The Cardinals, skippered by Johnny Keane, stole the National League title on the season's final day after Philadelphia blew a 6½ game lead with 12 games to go.

It was the second time in team history the Yankees had made it to five straight World Series. Mickey Mantle, playing in his final Fall Classic, batted .333 with three home runs and eight runs batted in, and Bobby Richardson collected a record 13 hits in the Series. But the Cardinals were not impressed, prevailing in seven tense games behind the over-powering pitching of Bob Gibson, who won two Series games and struck out thirty-one Yankees in 27 innings.

The third game, after the teams had split the first two games in St. Louis, proved to be Mantle's defining World Series moment. The score was tied 1-1 going into the bottom of the ninth inning. Mantle was due to lead off against knuckle-balling relief pitcher Barney Schultz. As Mantle was watching Schultz warm up, he turned to Elston Howard, the on-deck batter, and said, "You might as well go on in. I'm going to hit the first pitch I see out of the park." Sure enough, Mantle deposited Schultz's first pitch into the third deck of the right-field grandstand to win Game 3 and break a tie with Babe Ruth for career Series homers. The Mick hit two more in the games that followed to set a mark of 18 Series homers that will be hard to match.

The long ball was a big St. Louis weapon, too. Ken Boyer's grand slam was all the runs the Cards needed in a 4-3 victory in Game 4, and Tim McCarver's 10th inning home run to win Game 5 gave the Cardinals a three-games-to-two Series edge heading back to St. Louis. The home runs continued to fly in Game 6 for the Yanks, as Joe Pepitone's grand slam forced a deciding seventh game. The Bombers produced three home runs off Gibson in Game 7, but it was not enough to win the Series. Pitching on two days rest, Gibson outlasted rookie Mel Stottlemyre, hanging on for a 7-5 win and the Cardinals first championship since 1946. St. Louis general manager Branch Rickey was ecstatic. "It's the most champagne I've had in four years," he said in the celebratory locker room. "I'd rather beat the Yankees than any other team in baseball."

In a stunning development, both World Series managers were no longer with their ball clubs after Game 7. The Yankees ownership was unhappy with Berra's performance and fired him, while Keane quit the Cardinals and then became the Yankees' skipper. The fact that neither pennant-winning manager would return to their old club was an odd twist.

The loss turned out to be an omen for the great Yankees dynasty that started in the 1920s with Ruth and Gehrig and peaked from 1947 to 1964. During those eighteen postwar seasons, the Yankees won 15 A.L. pennants and 10 World Series. But after never having to wait more than four years to reach a World Series, the Bronx Bombers did not make it back again for twelve years. It was the end of an era. Within two years, the Yankees would tumble all the way to last place.

Mickey Mantle (7), Elston Howard, left, and Tom Tresh (15) greet teammate Joe Pepitone at the home base after he hit a grand slam home run in the eighth inning of the sixth World Series game against the St. Louis Cardinals on October 14, 1964. Pepitone's home run forced a deciding seventh game. (AP Photo)

THE HARMONICA INCIDENT

The turning point of the 1964 season for the Yankees occurred not on the playing field, but on the team bus. It is infamously known as the "Harmonica Incident" and lives on today in Yankee folklore thanks to Mickey Mantle's mischievous ways.

The incident occurred on the afternoon of August 20, 1964. Despite having won four straight American League pennants, the injured-riddled Yankees were mired in third place. They had just been shut out for a fourth straight loss to the Chicago White Sox, dropping them 4½ games out of first place. The players were sitting inside the team bus, which was delayed leaving Comiskey Park, when backup infielder Phil Linz pulled out a harmonica and began playing "Mary Had a Little Lamb."

Yogi Berra, in his first season as manager, instructed Linz to put the instrument away. "You lose four straight and act like we won the pennant," Berra shouted, according to reporters who had accompanied the players on the bus. Linz apparently didn't hear Berra, so he turned to teammate Mickey Mantle and asked, "What did he say?"

"He said to play louder," Mantle said.

So Linz continued to toot away, sparking an irate Berra to leave his seat at the front of the bus and charge at Linz. It was the angriest Linz had ever seen Berra, who was stewing over the string of losses. "I thought he was going to hit me," Linz said. "He just lost it." Linz tossed the harmonica to Berra, who slapped it in midair. It hit first baseman Joe Pepitone on the knee, tearing his pants and scratching his leg. (Pepitone, ever the cutup, cried out, "Corpsman, corpsman, I'm wounded!")

The Yankees, losers of 12 of their last 18 games at the time of the incident, then went on a tear. They won 30 of their final 41 games and captured the American League pennant. Some followers of the team believed the harmonica incident fueled the winning surge. But when the Yankees lost the World Series in seven games to the St. Louis Cardinals, Berra was fired, and his angry explosion over Linz's harmonica playing was cited as a factor that the manager had lost control of his players.

The incident turned out well for Linz, who hit two home runs during the 1964 series. Although Linz was ultimately fined two hundred dollars by Berra, the publicity led to a rewarding endorsement contract with the Hohner Harmonica Company. An advertisement on the back cover of the 1965 Yankee yearbook featured

Part Three

Linz, in a Yankee uniform and cap, with a harmonica at his mouth. The caption read: "Play It, Phil."

"If people remember me at all," said Linz, a seven-year backup infielder who hit .235 with 11 homers, "they remember me as a harmonica player, because I sure wasn't too good of a baseball player."

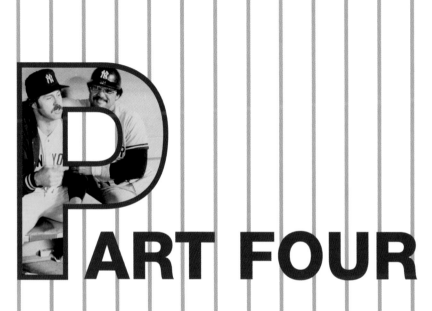

PART FOUR

THE BRONX ZOO

1973

The Boss

George M. Steinbrenner III, a ship builder from Cleveland, led a group of investors in buying the New York Yankees from the Columbia Broadcasting System (CBS) in 1973 for a bargain-basement price of $8.7 million. "It's the best buy in sports today," said Steinbrenner, who also vowed to leave the daily operation of the baseball team to others.

"I won't be active in the day-to-day operations of the club at all," he said the day the sale was announced at Yankee Stadium. "I can't spread myself so thin. I've got enough headaches with my shipping company."

The once-proud Yankees franchise was floundering, following nine consecutive losing seasons and dwindling attendance. Aided by the coming of free agency, Steinbrenner would return the Yankees to prominence. Under his tenure—the longest ownership in team history—the Yankees won 11 pennants and seven World Series championships.

The man known simply as "The Boss" was known for several things, most notably an intolerance for losing and a short fuse. He hired and fired managers with abandon, especially early in his ownership. The fiery Billy Martin was re-hired five times!

In 1974, Commissioner Bowie Kuhn suspended Steinbrenner from baseball ownership for two years after The Boss was indicted for making illegal contributions to President Richard Nixon's re-election campaign and then covering it up. The suspension was lifted after 15 months, with Steinbrenner returning to the Yankees in 1976. Under Steinbrenner's watchful eye, the Yankees won three consecutive pennants beginning in 1976, and won the 1977 and 1978 World Series, albeit in a turbulent environment dubbed by pitcher Sparky Lyle as "The Bronx Zoo."

In 1990, Steinbrenner was suspended again, this time for life, by Commissioner Fay Vincent after the owner had hired a known gambler to dig up dirt on outfielder Dave Winfield after Winfield didn't perform in the clutch to Steinbrenner's liking. Steinbrenner was reinstated in 1993, and the Yankees were a model franchise, and Steinbrenner a model owner, thereafter.

The Yankees returned to the postseason in 1995, the first of 13 consecutive postseason appearances. By then, Steinbrenner had mellowed, allowing Joe Torre to remain in the manager's office for 12 seasons, and leaving personnel decisions to his organizational brain trust. With World Series titles in 1996, 1998, 1999, 2000 and 2009, the Yankees have won 27 world championships, more than any franchise.

In addition to the team's on-field success during Steinbrenner's ownership reign, the Yankees topped the American League in attendance for a record eight straight seasons from 2003 to 2010. The Yankees are also the only franchise in baseball history to draw more than 4 million fans at home in four consecutive seasons (2005-08).

The Yankees, according to *Forbes* magazine, are the most valuable team in baseball, now worth nearly $3.5 billion, thanks to Steinbrenner's astute business tactics. He was the first owner to sell broadcast rights of his team's games to cable television, an idea which has grown into the Yankees' own YES Network. Steinbrenner spearheaded a renovation of Yankee Stadium in the mid 1970s and then oversaw the building of a new Yankee Stadium that opened for the 2009 season, keeping the team in the Bronx.

In 2007, The Boss, age seventy-seven and in failing health, ceded control of the team to his two sons, Hank and Hal. George Steinbrenner died in 2010 after thirty-seven years as principal owner, during which time the Yankees posted a major league-best .566

Yankees owner George Steinbrenner had complicated relationships with his managers. Here he is with skipper Joe Torre before Game 1 of the ALCS in 1998. (AP Photo/Adam Nadel)

winning percentage. Steinbrenner's tenure at the helm is the longest of any other New York Yankees owner by thirteen years. (Colonel Jacob Ruppert owned the Yankees from 1915 to 1939, a total of twenty-four years.) Steinbrenner's reign brought a level of stability to the Yankees that other teams only dream about. Since the Steinbrenner family took over the Yankees, the other twenty-nine major league teams have had over 100 owners while the Yankees have had just one.

1973
The First Designated Hitter

Ron Blomberg was the number one overall pick in the 1967 amateur draft and he made his New York Yankees debut on September 10, 1969. But he made baseball history when he stepped into the batter's box on Opening Day in 1973. The Yankees were playing the Boston Red Sox in Fenway Park, and the American League was unveiling its new designated hitter rule. The "designated pinch-hitter" is a player used as an extra batter who usually hits in the pitcher's spot in the batting order. In the first inning, Blomberg became the first designated hitter (DH) to bat in a major league game.

More than four decades have passed since Blomberg's momentous at-bat, and his claim to fame—as well as the DH rule—is here to stay.

"It's incredible," Blomberg says of his notoriety. "I was an answer in *Trivial Pursuit*. I was a question on *Jeopardy!* And it all happened because I pulled a hamstring in spring training [in 1973]."

Indeed, it was a stroke of fate that made Blomberg the first designated hitter. Yankees manager Ralph Houk had not once tried Blomberg, a first baseman, as the DH during spring training, opting instead for Felipe Alou or Johnny Callison. But days before the season started, Blomberg suffered a slight pull in his right hamstring.

"Ralph told me that if it was cold in Boston on Opening Day, he might put me in the lineup as the DH to keep me from really hurting myself," said Blomberg.

So on April 6, 1973, the temperature in Boston was in the low 40s, but 25-mile-per-hour wind gusts made it feel much colder. When the Yankees' lineup card was posted, Blomberg was listed as the designated hitter. Immediately, the sportswriters flocked around him to ask how he liked being the DH. "I don't know," Blomberg answered, "I've never done it before."

At game time, the wind played a key role in Blomberg's destiny. After Red Sox starting pitcher Luis Tiant retired the first two Yankees batters, Matty Alou hit what should have been an inning-ending routine fly ball. But the wind currents played havoc with the baseball, and it dropped in front of centerfielder Reggie Smith for a double. Tiant then walked Bobby Murcer and Graig Nettles to load the bases, setting the stage for Blomberg.

He approached the plate and dug in. "Why are you the designated hitter?" Red Sox catcher Carlton Fisk asked Blomberg. "I thought the DH is supposed to be some guy sixty years old."

"Sometimes," joked Blomberg, "my body does feel sixty."

Tiant still had trouble finding his control, and he walked Blomberg, forcing in a Yankees run. The first major league appearance by a designated hitter was not an official at-bat, although Blomberg was credited with a run batted in. The DH rule wasted no time adding offense to the game.

"When I got to first base, I looked at the umpire and I didn't know what to do," explained Blomberg, who was unsure about his status as a DH once on base. "He told me to just do what I always do."

The Yankees scored twice more in the inning to take a 3-0 lead. When the side was retired, Blomberg instinctively remained on the base paths, waiting for a teammate to bring him his glove. It never arrived.

"Our pitcher [Mel Stottlemyre] was already warming up and Felipe Alou [the first baseman] was throwing grounders for infield practice when I hustled off the field. [Coach] Elston Howard told me to sit down next to him on the bench."

The Yankees' 3-0 lead was short-lived, and they eventually lost 15-5. The Boston batting star was Fisk, who hit two home runs, including a grand slam, and drove in six runs. The only Red Sox regular who didn't get a hit was their DH, Orlando Cepeda.

For the record, Blomberg went 1 for 3 on the day. He walked, got a broken-bat single, lined out and flied out. Still, he was the media's focal point in the clubhouse when the game ended.

"We lose 15-5, and what seemed like 100 reporters were asking me questions about being the first DH," said Blomberg. "That's when I realized that I was a part of history."

Yankees public relations director Marty Appel never doubted that history was in the making. He grabbed Blomberg's bat and shipped it to the Hall of Fame, where the Louisville Slugger is still prominently displayed. The wood Blomberg used to get his broken-bat single, ironically, ended up in the garbage heap.

Only in baseball's America, Blomberg is fond of saying, could a nice Jewish boy from Georgia leave a legacy in Cooperstown. But if Blomberg had not hurt his leg, and if the weather had not been cold, and if a wind-blown fly ball had not fallen safely, Cepeda, not the Boomer (as he was known), might have been the first DH to bat.

"People might have forgotten about me if I wasn't the first DH," said Blomberg. "There aren't too many firsts in baseball, and I'm a first. The first DH. I went into the Hall of Fame through the back door. Who ever thought that one at-bat could be so important?"

By early July of '73, Blomberg was batting over .400 when *Sports Illustrated* featured him and teammate Bobby Murcer on the magazine's cover with the billing "Pride of the Yankees." Blomberg finished his best season ever batting .329 in 301 at-bats with 12 homers and 57 runs batted in.

Blomberg served as the Yankees' DH in 56 games in 1973, and he projected the proper attitude about his role, "If Ralph (Houk) thinks I can help most by being the DH, then it's all right with me," he said. "I love to play (in the field), but I know that I'm a better hitter than anything else."

In the three years that followed, knee and shoulder injuries limited the Boomer's playing time, and the Yankees released him after the '76 season. He attempted a comeback in 1978 with the Chicago White Sox, after a one-year hiatus, but his stroke had disappeared.

Blomberg hit with little power and his .231 average dropped his lifetime batting average from .301 to .293. At age thirty, the Boomer's career was over.

"I'm happy I gave it one last shot," said Blomberg, "but it did cost me my .300 lifetime average. Maybe then I'd be remembered for something else besides being the first DH. But at least I have that."

1974

Reeling in a Catfish

It certainly was a Happy New Year in 1975 for Yankees fans. Dangling the first multi-million dollar contract as bait, New York Yankees owner George Steinbrenner landed the most celebrated catch in free agent history, signing the former Oakland Athletics pitching ace Jim "Catfish" Hunter, on December 31, 1974. Steinbrenner, just two years into his ownership reign, was announcing his intention to build a winner for New York.

After leading the Athletics to a third straight World Series title and winning the Cy Young Award following the 1974 season, a financial dispute with Oakland owner Charles O. Finley led Hunter to declare himself a free agent—two years before the beginning of official free agency. The dispute stemmed from a contract issue regarding deferred payments. The previous winter, Hunter and Finley agreed on a two-year contract for $100,000 a year, but each year only $50,000 was to be paid to Hunter as straight salary; the remaining $50,000 was to be paid to a life insurance fund. The straight-salary part was paid routinely, but the insurance payments were not made because it would involve unfavorable tax consequences for Finley. Hunter contended Finley did not honor the agreement and therefore voided the contract. Finley said there was no contract violation, just disagreement over interpretation. Undeterred, Hunter filed for free agency when Finley refused to pay. An arbitrator, Peter Seitz, ruled in Hunter's favor at a hearing on December 15, 1974, and declared Hunter a free agent.

The twenty-eight-year-old pitcher was a prized free agent catch. Hunter had 106 victories over the last five seasons with the A's and was the reigning American League Cy Young Award winner with a career-best 25 wins. As expected, an incredible bidding war among at least twenty teams broke out for Hunter's services for the 1975 season as team officials descended on the North Carolina law offices of Cherry, Cherry and Flythe in North Carolina, near Hunter's home in Hertford. But in the end, it was New York owner George Steinbrenner who swooped in to grab Hunter with the richest deal in baseball at the time. Hunter signed with the Yankees on New Year's Eve for an unprecedented $3.5 million package over five years. The era of the big-contract superstar free agent had officially begun.

"To be a Yankee is a thought in everyone's head and mine," Hunter said. "Just walking into Yankee Stadium, chills run through you. I believe there was a higher offer, but no matter how much money offered, if you want to be a Yankee, you don't think about it."

Hunter won 23 games in his first season in the Bronx, in 1975, leading the American League with 328 innings, and no one since has come close to matching his amazing 30 complete games. Without its ace, Finley's A's would fall to last place by 1977. The Yankees, meanwhile, were revitalized by their new addition. With one stroke of the pen, the Yankees became immediate World Series contenders. Hunter would lead them to three consecutive pennants and back-to-back World Series titles in 1977–78, restoring the Bronx Bombers to the top of the baseball world. Catfish was a World Series starter in each of the team's three Fall Classic appearances.

Hunter was just 63-53 in five seasons for the New York Yankees from 1975 to 1979. But numbers don't measure Hunter's importance to the Yankees. "You started our success," Steinbrenner told Hunter upon the pitcher's induction to the Hall of Fame in 1987. "You were the first to teach us how to win."

During spring training of 1978, doctors diagnosed Hunter as a diabetic, but he still went on to be a twelve-game winner and the winning pitcher in Game 6 of New York's World Series-clinching victory over the Dodgers. Arm trouble forced Hunter to retire at age thirty-three in 1979, or at least that's what his Hall of Fame plaque states. Hunter has a different explanation: "I wanted to start spending time with my family, and I told the Yankees when I signed that I would only play for five years," adding, "I had no arm problems when I retired."

When he was inducted into the Hall of Fame in his third year of eligibility in 1987, Hunter was surprised.

"I didn't think I would make it," he said. "I figured I wasn't good enough. I figured the people in there were like gods."

To which commissioner Peter Ueberroth noted, "Catfish Hunter had the distinction of playing for both Charlie Finley and George Steinbrenner, which is enough to put a player in the Hall of Fame."

Hunter became the first player born after World War II to gain a spot in Cooperstown. He died in 1999 at age fifty-three from amyotrophic lateral sclerosis, the same disease that took the life of another Yankees legend, Lou Gehrig.

1976

Chambliss Delivers

The remodeled Yankee Stadium was unveiled in 1976, and like in 1923, the New York Yankees opened their new stadium in grand style by reaching the World Series. New York first baseman Chris Chambliss sent the hometown fans into frenzy with a dramatic home run in the last of the ninth inning against the Kansas City Royals in the decisive Game 5 of the American League Championship Series to deliver a pennant to the Bronx for the first time since 1964.

The 1976 Yankees acted like the Yankees of old, winning 97 games to run away with the A.L. east division title by a 10-game cushion. The Yankees were four seasons into the ownership reign of George Steinbrenner and in the first full season with former Yankee second baseman and 1953 World Series hero Billy Martin as manager. "The Yankees belonged in the World Series," Martin said before the series. "That's the way it was when I played with the Yankees and that's the way I want it to be as I manage the Yankees."

The Yankees and Royals were tied at two games apiece and the score was knotted at 6-6 in the decisive game when Chambliss stepped in to face Kansas City reliever Mark Littell to open the last of the ninth. Before Chambliss could hit, the game was delayed while the Yankee Stadium grounds crew picked up beer bottles and rolls of toilet paper thrown from the stands. As Chambliss waited, public address announcer Bob Sheppard cautioned the crowd of over 58,000 not to throw debris onto the playing field.

"I was a little anxious," Chambliss said of the delay. "It was cold, too. That was a trying little time there." Littell was annoyed by the delay, too. Finally, Chambliss stepped into the box. "I knew Littell was going to throw a fastball," he said. Littell delivered a high inside fastball, and Chambliss, who was 10 for 20 with 7 RBIs in the playoffs, belted the pitch high and deep toward the right field wall.

Yankees first baseman Chris Chambliss celebrates after hitting the game-winning home run in the bottom of the ninth inning during the fifth and deciding game of the American League Championship Series against the Kansas City Royals at Yankee Stadium, October 14, 1976. Chambliss's shot was the first pennant-winning walkoff home run in Yankees history. (AP Photo/Ray Stubblebine)

"Sometimes you'll see players drop their bats at home plate to admire the ball as it goes out of the park," said Chambliss. "They know they hit it so well, it's a home run from the moment it leaves their bats. This wasn't one of those. The ball I hit was more what you would call a towering drive with a lot of height, but I didn't know if it had enough distance to make it out. When I hit the ball, it looked as if the Royals right fielder had a bead on it. He moved back as if he was going to catch it. But at the very last second, he backed into the wall and the ball cleared it."

When Chambliss smashed Littell's first pitch over the right-field wall, it touched off a wild celebration at Yankee Stadium. New York fans had grown accustomed over the years to seeing their Yankees win pennants almost at will. But New York's eleven-season drought from 1965 to 1975 was its longest since winning its first American League title in 1921. And so, when Chambliss' blast landed in the right-field bleachers, it triggered a mad rush as thousands of joyous fans poured onto the field in celebration to mob their new hero as he circled the bases. Chambliss, in fact, was knocked to the ground by overzealous fans between second and third base. "I was in the middle of a mass of people, and when I fell to the ground, it was scary," he said. Chambliss was escorted off the field and into the clubhouse, then returned later to touch home plate.

Despite Chambliss' heroics, the world championship trophy remained in Cincinnati for another season. The defending champion Reds had little trouble dispatching the Yankees in four games in the World Series. Cincinnati second baseman Joe Morgan homered in the bottom of the first inning of Game 1, and the Reds never looked back, steamrolling to 5-1, 4-3, 6-2, and 7-2 victories. Game 2 at Cincinnati's Riverfront Stadium psychologically deflated the Yanks. On the mound was their ace pitcher, Jim "Catfish" Hunter, with the score tied 3-3 going into the bottom of the ninth inning. With two outs and nobody on, speedy Ken Griffey, Sr. bounced a ground ball to Yankee shortstop Fred Stanley, who threw wildly for a two-base error. After an intentional walk to the next batter, Joe Morgan, Cincinnati first baseman Tony Perez lined Hunter's first pitch into left field for the game winning hit.

Reds designated hitter Dan Driessen—this was the first World Series allowing the new DH rule—went 3 for 3 with a home run and a double in Game Three at Yankee Stadium. Following the 6-2 defeat manager Martin vowed the Yankees would win the next four in a row. The Yankees led only once in the Series, when they took a 1-0 lead in the first inning of the fourth, and final, game. Cincinnati erased that deficit and went on to win 7-2, sweeping the Yankees.

"This won't happen again," said Martin. "We'll be a better team next year."

Reds catcher Johnny Bench was the star of the World Series, batting .533 with two home runs and six runs batted in. The one real bright spot for the Yankees was catcher Thurman Munson, who hit .529, with a Series-best nine hits, including hits in his last six at-bats. Jim Mason, pinch-hitting in Game 3 for the Yankees, hit a home run, becoming the first player to homer in his only Series at-bat.

Part Four

1977

Mr. October

When Reggie Jackson arrived in New York for the 1977 season, he instantly made friends with Yankees fans that had been starving for a winner since 1964. But Jackson wasn't liked by all of his teammates. Years before he arrived in New York, Jackson boasted that if he were ever to play in the intense media glare of that city, he would end up with a candy bar named after him. He did.

"I didn't come to New York to be a star," Reggie once said. "I brought my star with me."

The tempestuous Jackson combined with fiery manager Billy Martin and other stubborn and egotistical personalities in the Yankees organization to form a volatile mix that threatened to undermine the team's fortunes. The clubhouse was dubbed "The Bronx Zoo" because of the constant bickering among Jackson, Martin, catcher Thurman Munson, owner George Steinbrenner, and others. In the end, though, the team fed off the atmosphere to win its first World Series in fifteen years.

New York, which had won 100 games during the regular season to edge the Baltimore Orioles and Boston Red Sox by two-and-a-half games in the American League's eastern division, outlasted the Kansas City Royals in a taut pennant race. The Yankees scored three runs in the ninth inning of the fifth and final game to win 5-3 and wrest the pennant from the Royals' clutches.

Jackson struggled against Kansas City's pitching in the league championship series (hitting just .125 with one run batted in, and zero home runs), but he made the World Series against the Los Angeles Dodgers his personal stage, on which he batted .450 with five home runs and eight runs batted in. The Yankees won in six games, and Jackson's performance in the finale—when he blasted three home runs—was one of the most memorable in World Series history.

Jackson's reputation as a star in the postseason earned him the nickname "Mr. October," and his dramatic play in game six of the 1977 World Series was a signature performance.

Reggie Jackson blasts his third home run during the sixth and final game of the World Series at Yankee Stadium in New York on October 18, 1977. (AP Photo)

After receiving a base on balls in his first plate appearance that night against the Dodgers, Jackson belted a two-run home run off Los Angeles staring pitcher Burt Hooton in the fourth inning to put the Yankees ahead for good. The next inning, he slugged another two-run homer off reliever Elias Sosa that left the park in the blink of an eye. "I overwhelmed that baseball by the sheer force of my will," said Jackson.

Then, in the eighth, with the Yankees' title well in hand, he punctuated the night with a solo home run off Charlie Hough that landed deep into the far-away centerfield bleachers. The beauty of Jackson's performance was that he blasted each of his three home runs on the first pitch against three different pitchers.

"I must admit," said Dodgers first baseman Steve Garvey, "when Reggie hit his third home run and I was sure nobody was looking, I applauded in my glove."

As Jackson crossed home plate, the 56,407 exuberant hometown fans paid tribute to one of the greatest individual performances in baseball history by screaming, "Reg-gie, Reg-gie," until their hero popped out of the dugout for a curtain call, nodding to the appreciative crowd. He became the second player, after Babe Ruth in 1928, to hit three homers in a Series game. His five homers for the Series, including four in a row, were also a record.

It was no surprise that Jackson was such a World Series star, because he thrived in the spotlight. For his career, Jackson batted .357 with 10 home runs in 98 World Series at bats. He was the World Series Most Valuable Player in 1973 (while with the Oakland

Athletics) and 1977, set a career record for slugging percentage (.755), and played on five championship teams.

Jackson was an all-or-nothing showman who belted 563 career home runs, but also struck out an incredible 2,597 times, the most in major league history. He helped carry his teams to ten playoff appearances in a twelve-year span from 1971 to 1982, but he also put off teammates and fans with his bragging.

When Jackson signed a $3 million contract with the Yankees in 1977, he became baseball's highest-paid player and proclaimed himself "the straw that stirs the drink" in New York. He quickly alienated established Yankees stars with the remark. Eventually, though, he may have proved himself right.

REGGIE! BAR NONE

Reggie Jackson famously boasted that if he ever played in New York, they'd name a candy bar after him. Sure enough, after his memorable performance in the 1977 World Series, he got his wish. Manufactured by Standard Brands Confectionary, the "Reggie!" candy bar was a round, 25-cent patty of chocolate-covered caramel and peanuts. Cracked teammate Catfish Hunter: "When you unwrap a 'Reggie!' bar, it tells you how good it is."

Reggie Jackson embraces Catfish Hunter in the eighth inning of Game Six of the 1978 World Series. (AP Photo)

Prior to the 1978 Yankees home opener, Standard Brands handed out free "Reggie!" bars as a sales promotion gimmick to the 44,667 fans who passed through the turnstiles. The home opener also marked the day that Roger Maris ended his twelve-year exile by returning to the Bronx. In a pre-game ceremony, Maris and Mickey Mantle raised the team's first world championship flag in fifteen years.

In the game's first inning, Reggie Jackson, who had homered on his last three swings of the 1977 World Series at Yankee Stadium, connected again on his first cut of the home season, smashing a three-run homer off Chicago's Wilbur Wood in the Yankees' 4-2 win over the White Sox.

When Reggie took his position in right field to start the second inning, the fans threw thousands of "Reggie!" bars onto the field in tribute. The game was delayed about five minutes for groundskeepers to gather the candy.

Part Four

1978

Louisiana Lightning

Yankee Stadium has played host to eleven no-hitters, including three perfect games, but it is safe to say that no pitcher was more dominant in the Bronx than Ron Guidry on June 17, 1978, for on that memorable night, he turned the California Angels' bats into sawdust.

Guidry struck out a team record 18 batters, including nine in a row. The twenty-seven—year-old from Lafayette, Louisiana, allowed four hits on the way to a 4-0 victory. At the time, it was the most strikeouts ever in baseball history by a left-handed pitcher in a nine-inning game. (Seattle's Randy Johnson since surpassed the mark by striking out 19 batters in a game twice during the 1997 season.)

Although Guidry struck out two California batters in the first inning, he feared a struggle. "Believe it or not, I didn't think I was going to get out of the first inning of that game because I couldn't get my slider in the strike zone," said Guidry. "I kept bouncing it, and when I got it over the plate, it was always high. I couldn't throw my fastball for strikes when I was warming up either. I saw (Yankees relief pitcher) Sparky Lyle when I came in from the bullpen, and I asked him, 'What's the earliest you've ever come into a game? I don't feel like I have good stuff tonight.' And Sparky said to me, 'You've got good stuff. It's just a little high. Just go out there, and eventually, it will come.'

"When I went out in the third inning, things started to change," Guidry continued. "The Angels were just swinging and missing. When I threw balls down the middle of the plate, they were taking. When they'd swing, it would be out of the strike zone. I had them off-balance. After the third inning, guys were just striking out."

Somehow, despite his wiry 5-foot-11, 160-pound frame, Guidry could throw a fastball 95 miles per hour, and his slider handcuffed and tormented right-handed hitters. "He caught a lot of teams by surprise because of his size," recalled third baseman Graig Nettles. "They didn't expect him to throw that hard."

Ron Guidry in action at Yankee Stadium in 1977. (AP Photo)

On this night, Guidry's fastball pounded the catcher's mitt so loudly that the television announcer, Phil Rizzuto, began calling him "Louisiana Lightning."

The Yankees scored all their runs in the first three innings. After that it was zeroes for both teams, and the way Guidry was pitching, they could have played 20 innings and the Angels weren't scoring. Through six innings he had 14 strikeouts—meaning that only four of the 18 outs had come on balls that were put in play.

By the time Guidry was done, he had struck out the side three times and had struck out every Angels batter at least once. The victims: Bobby Grich twice; Rick Miller once; Dave Chalk twice; Joe Rudi four times; Don Baylor twice; Ron Jackson once; Merv Rettenmund once; Brian Downing twice; and Ike Hampton three times. As California's Joe Rudi, who fanned four times, said afterward, "If you saw that pitching too often, there would be a lot of guys doing different jobs."

This was also the game that began the Yankee Stadium tradition of fans getting up on their feet and rhythmically clapping for a strikeout whenever the batter gets two strikes against him. On this night against the Angels, the boisterous hometown crowd of 33,162 kept getting up on its feet every time Guidry got two strikes on a California batter. And more times than not, he rewarded them with the third strike.

"When they start hollering and screaming, you just get pumped up that much higher and you try harder," said Guidry, who was known as Gator to his teammates. "I felt I disappointed them when a guy hit a ball with two strikes. I thought I made a mistake."

Part Four

To this day, whenever an opposing batter gets two strikes against him, Yankee fans will rise to their feet and methodically clap for a strikeout, a tradition since June 17, 1978.

Guidry improved to 11-0 with his win over the Angels. He would win his first 13 decisions of the 1978 season and go on to finish 25-3 with nine shutouts. His 25th win came in the Yankees' victory over the Red Sox in the one-game playoff at Fenway Park to win the American League eastern division title. Then the Yankees went on to win their second World Series title in a row. In postseason honors, Guidry won the Cy Young Award and was runner-up to Boston's Jim Rice in the Most Valuable Player voting.

1978

Bullpen Aces

By the early 1970s every team began to see the importance of having an ace relief pitcher in its bullpen—a closer—to nail down the final outs and win a game. To this end, it was the acquisition of two relief pitchers to serve the closer's role that proved pivotal to locking down two consecutive World Series triumphs for the Yankees in 1977 and 1978. The first, Sparky Lyle, was transacted by shrewd trade; the other, Rich "Goose" Goosage, by free agent signing.

Lyle was a gregarious and mustachioed left-handed reliever. Acquired in 1972 for first baseman Danny Cater in what turned out to be yet another lopsided trade with the Boston Red Sox, Lyle relied on a sharp-breaking slider to save 141 games in seven seasons with the Yankees from 1972 to 1978. He never started a major league game. Though Dave Righetti and Mariano Rivera would surpass his save numbers, Lyle was instrumental in helping the Yankees return to their winning ways in the mid 1970s.

In his first season in the Bronx, Lyle set the American League record with 35 saves (and nine wins), while recording a 1.92 earned run average in over 100 innings pitched. When Yankees manager Ralph Houk would signal to the bullpen late in games during the 1972 season, Lyle would make an electric appearance. Marty Appel, the team's publicist, remembered: "Lyle would arrive in the Datsun bullpen car, throw open the door, jump out of it with fire in his eyes, throw his warm-up jacket to the waiting batboy, and storm to the mound. A few quick warm-ups and then he'd stare in at [catcher Thurman] Munson, waiting for the batter to dare to step up."

To further inspire the already raucous crowd, Appel wanted a triumphant musical accompaniment to play over the public address system during Lyle's warm-ups. He selected Sir Edgar Elgar's graduation march *Pomp and Circumstance* in what may have officially begun the era of entrance music for relievers.

"His entrances were so theatrical," Appel said. "The confidence, the body language, the whole thing had a bit of drama to it."

Lyle saved 27 games in 1973, and posted a career-best 1.66 ERA in 1974. He led the AL with 23 saves in 1976 as the Yankees won their first pennant in 12 years. In 1977, Lyle was even better, pitching an astounding 137 relief innings, winning 13 games with 26 saves (second in the A.L.), and becoming the first relief pitcher to win the Cy Young Award. He then added a win in the World Series as the Yankees beat the Los Angeles Dodgers in six games for their first title in fifteen years.

Thurmon Munson congratulates Sparky Lyle, right, after the Yankees defeated Kansas City Royals, 5-3, in third American league playoff game at Yankee Stadium on October 12, 1976. (AP Photo)

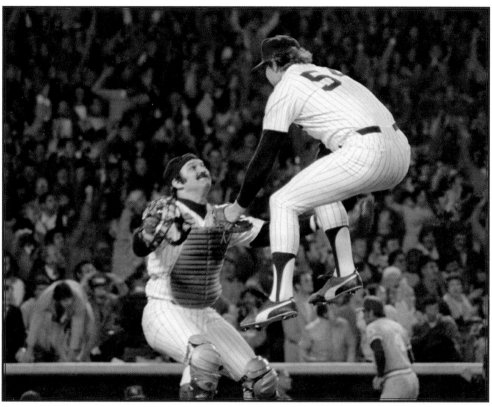

Two years later, on October 7, 1978, Munson and Goose Gossage celebrate after the Yankees again defeated the Royals to earn another trip to the World Series. (AP Photo/Richard Drew)

The Yankees signed Goose Gossage as a free agent in 1978 and he inherited the closer role from Lyle, the previous year's Cy Young winner, prompting third baseman Graig Nettles to tell Lyle he had gone from "Cy Young to Sayonara." Gossage made an immediate impact with the Yankees, winning 10 games and saving 27 more. Gossage was a workhorse; in 1978 he pitched 134 innings, fourth-highest on the staff. Then he saved the American League Eastern division playoff game against the Red Sox, and he was on the mound when the Yankees won the championship series against the Kansas City Royals and the World Series against the Los Angeles Dodgers.

The Goose was intimidating. He stood 6 foot 3, weighed 220 pounds, possessed a deathly scowl, and threw a fastball 100 miles per hour. Oh, and he detested his opponents. "My wife wouldn't know me out there," Gossage said. "If she ever came to the mound and talked to me, she'd divorce me. I don't like anybody with a bat in his hands because he's trying to hurt me with that thing. Hate is an ugly word, but I hate hitters."

Gossage spent most of the 1979 season on the disabled list following a locker room brawl with teammate Cliff Johnson, but he returned in 1980 to save a career-high 33 games. The Yankees won 103 regular season games, but were swept by the Kansas City

Royals in the championship series, with Gossage allowing the series-clinching home run to George Brett. Gossage was at his overpowering best during the strike-shortened 1981 season. Limited to just 32 appearances, Gossage still managed 20 saves and allowed only 22 hits in 47 innings to go with 48 strikeouts. He gave up only four earned runs for a 0.77 ERA, and didn't give up a run in 14 postseason innings. He saved all three wins over the Milwaukee Brewers during the divisional playoffs and both Yankees wins over the Dodgers in the World Series. His six years as the Yankees closer included four All-Star teams, 151 saves and a 2.14 earned run average. Prior to the 1984 season he signed with the San Diego Padres as a free agent and helped them reach the World Series for the first time. He was inducted into the Hall of Fame in 2008.

THE MERRY PRANKSTER

In 1979, after the Yankees traded Sparky Lyle to the Texas Rangers, Lyle published a book he had written about his experiences with the Yankees titled *The Bronx Zoo*. In the book we learn that in addition to being one of the most effective relief pitchers ever, Lyle was famous for his practical jokes. He once showed up at spring training camp with his pitching arm in a cast, just to scare his manager and teammates.

One of his favorite pranks was dropping his pants and sitting naked on a teammate's birthday cake. According to Red Sox pitcher Bill Lee, Lyle's cake-sitting was what prompted his trade from Boston to New York. "He sat on (Red Sox owner) Tom Yawkey's cake, and Yawkey found out," said Lee. "The next day Lyle is shipped off to the Yankees, and here comes Danny Cater—all because of sitting on a birthday cake."

Lyle claimed the reason he stopped sitting on cakes was because he feared someone might try to "put a needle in the cake" to teach him a painful lesson.

1978

Dent's Monster Moment

The Yankees' light-hitting shortstop Bucky Dent lifted a seventh-inning fly ball over the left-field wall at Boston's Fenway Park for a three-run homer, propelling the Yankees to a tension-filled 5-4 victory over the Red Sox in a one-game playoff that decided the 1978 American League east division championship. The home run by Dent, the number nine hitter in the lineup, broke the hearts of Red Sox Nation and gave validation to the "Curse of the Bambino."

After the teams finished the regular season tied atop the American League East with identical records of 99-63, they met at Boston's Fenway Park for one game to determine who would advance to the League Championship Series. The playoff became necessary when Boston won its final regular-season game and the Yankees lost to Cleveland.

The Red Sox broke out to a 2-0 lead against 24-game winner Ron Guidry on Carl Yastrzemski's second-inning home run and Jim Rice's sixth-inning RBI single. The Yankees could manage only two hits through six innings off Boston starter Mike Torrez, a Yankee free agent defector. But Chris Chambliss and Roy White singled in the seventh, and then Jim Spencer flew out. That brought up Dent, a .243 hitter who was allowed to bat only because the Yankees were short on extra infielders and could not pinch-hit.

Before his home run, Dent painfully fouled a ball off his foot. As he grimaced and hopped around in obvious pain, the trainer came out to take a look. With time out, Mickey Rivers, the on-deck batter, noticed that Dent was using a cracked bat. Rivers handed his bat to a batboy. "Give this to Bucky," said Rivers. "Tell him there are lots of hits in it. He'll get a home run."

Dent switched to the new bat despite being in the middle of an at-bat. Then it all happened. On the next pitch, Dent lifted a fly ball that seemed like a harmless pop-up to left field. Torrez swears he thought it was an easy out, just like most everyone else did. But the ball got a boost from the wind and settled onto the screen atop Fenway's Green Monster. It was a crushing blow; Dent had hit only four other homers all year. A double by Thurman Munson that scored Mickey Rivers provided another seventh-inning run for the Yankees, this one off of Bob Stanley, who had replaced Torrez.

Guidry, pitching on two days rest, didn't overwhelm the Red Sox, but he pitched well enough for the Yankees to have a 4-2 lead when he departed during the seventh inning. To preserve the lead, the Yankees called on relief ace Rich "Goose" Gossage. Soon he had a 5-2 lead on Reggie Jackson's decisive homer into the centerfield bleachers in the eighth. "It was a fast ball right over the plate," said Jackson, who detoured on his way back to the dugout to shake hands with Yankees owner George Steinbrenner.

The Red Sox rallied for two eighth-inning runs off Gossage to narrow the lead to 5-4 going into the ninth. With one out, Rick Burleson walked and Jerry Remy singled. Lou Piniella lost Remy's low liner in the glare of the late-afternoon sun, but the right fielder stabbed the ball with his glove, holding Burleson, the tying run, at second. To protect the lead, Gossage now had to face Jim Rice, who would be chosen the league's most valuable player because of his 46 homers and 139 runs batted in, and Carl Yastrzemski, the Red Sox future Hall of Famer.

"I wasn't worried out there," said Gossage, who earned his 27th save of the season. "If I got beaten I was going to lose on my own effort."

Rearing back, Gossage fired his fastball. Rice lifted a soft fly to Piniella, and then Yaz popped a high foul that Graig Nettles caught near third base to end the game. The Boston crowd sat in stunned disbelief. Dent, who was certainly not known as a power hitter, earned himself a place in Yankees lore—and the undying anger of Boston Red Sox fans everywhere—with an unlikely home run. The victory capped the Yankees' amazing comeback from a 14-game July deficit and earned them a chance to play the Kansas City Royals for the A.L. pennant.

1978

The Comeback Kids

The atmosphere in the New York Yankees' clubhouse in 1977 was known as the Bronx Zoo. That didn't change in 1978, and neither did the end result: a World Series championship for the Yankees in six games over the Los Angeles Dodgers. But this time, the Bombers overcame a two-games-to-none deficit by winning four straight games for the title. No team in Series history ever did that before.

The 1978 Yankees were no strangers to comebacks. Trailing the division-leading Red Sox by 14 games on July 19, the Yankees decided to make a change at the top. Manager Billy Martin was fired on July 24, and Bob Lemon replaced him. After Lemon took over, the Yankees responded to their new manager's easy-going style, shaving ten games off the Red Sox's lead in just over six weeks. But on September 6 the Yankees were still four games out with just 24 to go when they rolled into Fenway Park for an important four-game series.

The Yankees crushed the Red Sox by scores of 15-3, 13-2, 7-0, and 7-4. They had a seven-run inning, a six-run inning and a five-run inning. The Yankees outscored the Red Sox 42-9, out-hit them 67-21, and the Red Sox committed 12 errors to boot. Thurman Munson went 8 for 16. Ron Guidry threw a two-hitter in Game 3. When they left, after the Boston Massacre had been completed, the Yankees and Red Sox were all even in the standings with identical 86-56 records. The Bombers were rolling, and the Red Sox were reeling. Six days later at Yankee Stadium, Guidry fired another two-hit shutout over Boston and the Yankees rocketed three games in front of the staggering Red Sox.

That, however, was not the end of the Sox. Although the Yankees under Lemon would win 48 games and lose only 20, the Red Sox won 12 of their 14 final games and eight of them in a row. Winning their last game of the season while the Yankees were losing, the Red Sox forced a one-game playoff on Monday afternoon, October 2, at Fenway Park. It was the American League's first tie-breaking playoff game since 1948. Bucky Dent, the light-hitting shortstop, socked a startling three-run homer off Mike Torrez, in the seventh. The Yankees won the game, 5-4, and the division title.

In the postseason, the Yankees swatted away the pesky Kansas City Royals in the play-offs, but then lost the first two games of the World Series against the Los Angeles Dodgers, before storming back to win four straight and the series.

The Dodgers won the first two Series games in Los Angeles, 11-5 and 4-3. The second game featured a nerve-wracking confrontation between rookie pitcher Bob Welch and star outfielder Reggie Jackson, who made a career hitting in clutch situations such as this. In the ninth inning, with two runners on base and two outs, Jackson battled Welch over nine pitches, fouling off pitch after pitch, before fanning to end the game. "It was a great at-bat," said Jackson. "I enjoyed every pitch except the last."

The New Yorkers came home to the Bronx and won Game 3 behind the gutsy pitching of Guidry and the glove work of third baseman Graig Nettles. The Yankees needed ten innings to win Game 4 on Lou Piniella's game-winning hit. Jackson, ever in the middle of it all for the Yankees, impacted this game with his guile in the sixth inning, breaking up a double play by getting in the way of Bill Russell's throw to first. The ball hit Jackson in the thigh and caromed into right field, allowing a pivotal run to score. Dodgers' manager Tom Lasorda protested that Jackson intentionally stuck out his hip and interfered with the ball, but umpires weren't buying. "I didn't do anything but stand there," said Jackson.

New York blasted Los Angeles, 12-2, with an 18-hit barrage in Game 5, as rookie Jim Beattie pitched a complete game and Thurman Munson led the way with five runs batted in. In the decisive sixth game at Dodger Stadium, Catfish Hunter pitched seven innings and Rich Gossage shut the door on the Dodgers for a relatively easy 7-2 Yankees win and a second consecutive World Series championship. The big blow of the game was Jackson's 430-foot home run off Welch. Jackson hit .391 with two homers and eight RBIs in the Series, but the Yankees won the trophy on the hitting of two men at the bottom of the order: Brian Doyle, substituting at second base for the injured Willie Randolph, batted .438, and shortstop Bucky Dent, the Series Most Valuable Player, batted .417 with seven runs batted in.

1979

A Yankee Tragedy

The New York Yankees boast a legendary history, and sadly, that history has occasionally been touched by tragedy. On August 2, 1979, the Yankees' catcher and team captain, Thurman Munson, only thirty-two years old, was killed when the private plane he was piloting crashed shortly after takeoff near his home in Canton, Ohio. Munson had used a day off in the team's schedule to fly home to see his family. The unexpected death of the fiery, gruff, but very popular player shocked all New York baseball fans.

For nearly three decades, Munson's locker in Yankee Stadium remained unoccupied in tribute. When the team moved across the street to the new Yankee Stadium, Munson's

Thurman Munson in 1977. (AP Photo)

locker was carefully removed and transported from the old stadium and placed in the Yankees Museum, located up a ramp from the main level, near Gate 6.

Munson is still a revered figure in Yankees history. A seven-time All-Star selection, Munson hit for a .292 average over eleven seasons in Pinstripes and was at his best in the clutch, batting .357 in thirty postseason games between 1976 and 1978. Munson had a tough outer shell, but his teammates knew him as a leader, the heart and soul of three consecutive American League pennant winners and two World Series championship teams.

Drafted out of Kent State and after less than one season in the minors, Munson earned the starting catching job in spring training of 1970. That season, the Yankees won 93 games with a rookie catcher. It was their best season since 1964. Munson won the American League's Rookie of the Year Award, receiving 23 of 24 first-place votes. His .302 batting average ranked eighth best in the league. He was also quickly establishing himself as a quality defensive catcher, with a take-charge attitude.

Munson hit his stride in 1973, batting .301 with 74 runs batted in and a career-high 20 homers. He also won the first of three Gold Glove Awards for fielding excellence. In 1975, he hit .318 with 102 RBIs, establishing himself as one of the game's best clutch hitters. For his career, Munson batted .315 with runners in scoring position. He was also named the first Yankees team captain since Lou Gehrig four decades before. Like Gehrig, Munson is also remembered as a tragic figure.

In 1976, Munson earned the AL Most Valuable Player Award, finishing with a .302 average, 17 home runs and 105 runs batted in. The Yankees breezed to the A.L. East division title, and Munson hit .435 against the Kansas City Royals in the American League Championship Series. The Yankees returned to the World Series for the first time in 12 years, but the Cincinnati Reds swept the Yanks in four games. Munson did his part, however, batting .529 with nine hits in the series.

In 1977, the Yankees won a second straight pennant and Munson hit .308 with 18 homers and 100 RBIs. He was the first major leaguer in thirteen seasons and only the second catcher—to compile three straight seasons batting .300 while knocking in at least 100 runs. The Yankees won the World Series, beating the Los Angeles Dodgers in six games, for the franchise's first world title since 1962. As the defending champions in 1978, the Yankees trailed the division-leading Boston Red Sox by as many as 14 games in mid-July, but rallied with a great stretch run to win the division crown. New York faced the Kansas City Royals in the playoffs. In Game 3, with the series tied 1-1, Royals' third baseman George Brett hit a two-run home run—his third homer of the game off Yankees starting pitcher Jim "Catfish" Hunter—to put the Royals ahead, 5-4, in the top of the eighth inning. In the bottom of the inning, with a runner on base, Munson blasted a 430-foot shot over Yankee Stadium's Death Valley in the left-centerfield bullpen off Doug Byrd that proved to be the difference-maker for the Yankees. New York ousted Kansas City for the third consecutive year to advance to the World Series. The Yankees then overcame a two games to none deficit to the Dodgers by winning four straight games to capture the team's 22nd title.

Now thirty-one years old, the wear and tear of catching was eroding Munson's power. Playing on sheer guts during the 1978 season, he kept his batting average near .300, finishing at .297, but his production was way down, with six homers and 71 RBIs. The decline continued in 1979. On August 1st, after 97 games, Munson was hitting .288 with three homers and 39 RBIs. There was talk of retirement due to balky knees and an aching right shoulder. Most of all, he sorely missed his family. The life of a ballplayer is travel and time spent away from family. Munson found a way to spend more time with his wife, Diane, and their three children. He earned a pilot's license a few years earlier, and in 1979 he bought a twin-engine Cessna Citation. The Yankees finished a road trip in Chicago the night of August 1st. He flew home to spend the off-day with his family. He was practicing takeoffs and landings at the Akron-Canton airport. That afternoon, his plane crashed short of the runway and burst into flames. According to one of the passengers, in an interview conducted years later, all three initially survived the crash. Munson asked his passengers if they were ok. He lost consciousness soon after the crash and his friends were unable to extract him from the plane as it filled with smoke. Munson died, but miraculously, the two passengers survived.

The team flew to Ohio for the funeral service. Munson's close friends and teammates, Bobby Murcer and Lou Piniella, each delivered a tearful eulogy. The night of the funeral the Yankees returned to Yankee Stadium to play a game against the Baltimore Orioles. When the Yankees took the field, the catcher's box was left unmanned. Reggie Jackson wept openly during the pre-game ceremony. The game was one for the ages. The Yankees overcame a 4-0 deficit to win 5-4, with all the runs driven in by Bobby Murcer, who hit a three-run home run in the seventh inning and a two-run single in the ninth that gave the Yankees a dramatic walk-off victory. Murcer was so emotionally drained from the day that he nearly fainted on the field after the winning run crossed home plate.

The Yankees wore black armbands for the remainder of the season, and Munson's uniform No. 15 was retired. He was honored with a plaque in Monument Park in a commemorative ceremony in Yankee Stadium on September 20, 1980. The plaque reads: "Our captain and leader has not left us—today, tomorrow, this year, next . . . Our endeavors will reflect our love and admiration for him."

Part Four

1981

Down Goes Frazier

The New York Yankees made headlines during the 1981 World Series for all the wrong reasons. It appeared the Yankees would breeze to a Series triumph against the Los Angeles Dodgers when they won the first two games at Yankee Stadium by scores of 5-3 and 3-0. But then the roof caved in on the Yankees and they blew the next four games by scores of 5-4, 8-7, and 2-1 at Dodger Stadium, and by a lopsided 9-2 score in Game 6 at Yankee Stadium. Luckless Yankee relief pitcher George Frazier, done in by ground-ball singles and bloopers, was charged with the loss in three of those games, setting an ignominious record for most losses in a six-game Series. High-priced free agent Dave Winfield had troubles of his own in the Series as he managed just one single in 22 at-bats for an almost invisible .045 average, and was forever labeled "Mr. May" by owner George Steinbrenner for his ill-timed slump. And an angry Steinbrenner was allegedly involved in a fracas with Dodger fans in a Los Angeles hotel elevator after his team lost the fifth game.

The Series had gotten off to a promising start for the Yankees. Bob Watson hit a first-inning three-run home run to stake Yankees starter Ron Guidry in the opener. In Game 2, Tommy John, who had pitched for the Dodgers against the Yankees in the 1977 and 1978 Series and now was pitching for the Yankees, stymied his old teammates for seven innings and Rich Gossage completed the shutout for his second save in two days. "Every Series win is satisfying," said John, "but there was something very special getting back at the Dodgers after they decided I couldn't help them any more."

The Yankees had an aura of invincibility as the Series moved to Los Angeles, and the Dodgers were reeling. Manager Tom Lasorda turned to rookie sensation Fernando Valenzuela in Game 3, and although he allowed nine hits and seven walks, Valenzuela came away with the victory. "He didn't have good stuff, but it was one of the gutsiest performances I've ever seen," said Lasorda.

Frazier had won a game for the Yankees in the American League Championship Series against the Oakland Athletics, and during the regular season he compiled a 1.63 earned run average over 16 appearances. But in Game 3 at Dodger Stadium, relief pitcher Rudy May allowed the go-ahead run to score, which was charged to Frazier, saddling him with the loss.

The next day the Dodgers evened the series with another close win. This time, Frazier entered the game in the sixth inning of a 6-6 tie, and his bad luck continued. Dusty Baker reached base on an infield single and after Rick Monday's soft fly ball dropped for a double, Frazier was relieved by John, who allowed a sacrifice fly to Steve Yeager for the eventual go-ahead run, and another loss charged to Frazier. In Game 5, for the third day in a row, the Dodgers overcame a Yankees lead to grab a one-run victory. The Dodgers were one win away from the title, but Yankees manager Bob Lemon was not conceding.

"All we need is a two-game winning streak at home," said Lemon. "We've done that before."

The final game was tied 1-1 in the fourth inning when Lemon decided to pinch hit for John, his dependable starter, with two on and two out. The controversial decision backfired when Bobby Murcer flied out, and the Yankees did not score. Then Frazier came in to pitch, and again, he could not catch a break. An infield single, a sacrifice bunt, and another infield single gave the Dodgers the lead. Then the bullpen imploded as the Dodgers made it four wins in a row to take the Series, handing Frazier his third loss.

"It looks like the voodoo lady was against me in this Series," said Frazier.

In the locker room, Frazier answered every question from reporters after the game.

"I felt, at that time, I can go sit in the trainer's room, go hide somewhere, but what's that going to accomplish?" said Frazier, who retired as a broadcaster for the Colorado Rockies in 2015. "If I go with this and stand out at this locker and just answer every single question somebody fires at me, once it's over, I won't have to worry about it anymore."

Afterward, an irritated Steinbrenner issued a public apology to all Yankees fans. Despite the mea culpa, the 1981 World Series loss put the Yankees in a postseason funk that would keep them away from the World Series for fifteen seasons, the longest drought in team history since their first World Series in 1921.

For his part, Frazier did redeem himself in the 1987 World Series with the Minnesota Twins. He pitched two scoreless innings and helped the Twins win the championship.

Part Four

DAVE WINFIELD

On December 15, 1980, after a productive eight-year career with the San Diego Padres, Dave Winfield signed a ten-year free agent contract with the Yankees worth a reported $15 million, making him the highest-paid player in team sports history at the time.

In his first season in the Bronx, in 1981, Winfield helped the Yankees reach the World Series, finishing the strike-shortened season with a .294 batting average, 13 homers, and 68 runs batted in. He had an awful 1-for-22 performance in the World Series loss to the Los Angeles Dodgers, prompting owner George Steinbrenner to dub him "Mr. May." (Clutch hitting teammate Reggie Jackson was "Mr. October.") But Winfield came back strong the next season to hit a career best 37 homers. He also drove in over 100 runs, and would become the first Yankee to drive in at least 100 runs in a season for five consecutive seasons (1982-86) since Joe DiMaggio accomplished that feat over seven straight years (1936–42).

The infamous "Seagull Incident" occurred on August 4, 1983. Winfield was playing catch with a ball boy while warming up before the bottom of the fifth inning at Toronto's Exposition Stadium. A flock of seagulls had landed on the artificial turf. One of Winfield's tosses struck and killed a low-flying gull. "They say he hit the gull on purpose," said Yankees manager Billy Martin with tongue firmly in cheek. "They wouldn't say that if they'd seen the throws he'd been making. First time he hit the cutoff man all year."

But this was no laughing matter to Toronto police, who arrested Winfield in the Yankees locker room on a charge of animal cruelty. Winfield posted $500 bail and was released ninety minutes later. Charges were later dropped, as no criminal intent could be proven. "It's quite unfortunate that a fowl of Canada is no longer with us," said Winfield.

In 1984, Winfield and teammate Don Mattingly staged an exciting race for the season's best batting average. The race came down to the final game of the season. Winfield was leading Mattingly by two points (.341 to .339) entering the last game against Detroit. Winfield went 1 for 4 and his average dropped to .340, but Mattingly went 4 for 5 and pushed past Winfield with a .343 average to capture the batting title. In a display of mutual respect and good sportsmanship, the two players later walked off the field arm-in-arm.

Winfield missed the entire 1989 season with a herniated disk in his back and was traded to the Angels during the 1990 season before his contract expired. He joined the Toronto Blue Jays for the 1992 season and helped them reach the

World Series. In game six of the series, Winfield's two-out, two-run double in the 11th inning gave Toronto a 4-2 lead and, ultimately, the championship, over the Atlanta Braves.

With more than 3,000 hits, 450 home runs, and 200 stolen bases, Dave Winfield was one of baseball's greatest all-around outfielders for more than 20 seasons on a total of six big-league teams. He also won seven Gold Gloves for fielding excellence. He went into the Hall of Fame in 2001 wearing a Padres cap, and was honored with a day at Yankee Stadium, on August 19, 2001.

"I knew when I put on these pinstripes for the first time, it's a moment I'll never forget, and it's a moment that changed my life," Winfield said. "I put my heart and soul on this field every day. I'm truly proud to be remembered as a member of the Yankee family."

1983

The Pine Tar Game

The "Pine Tar Game" is certainly one of baseball's most bizarre and controversial finishes. On July 24, 1983, the Kansas City Royals were at Yankee Stadium to play the Yankees in just another regular season game. The Yankees were leading 4-3 in the top of the ninth inning with two outs when Royals third baseman George Brett smashed a two-run homer off Yankees relief pitcher Rich "Goose" Gossage, giving the Royals a 5-4 lead. Or so everyone in the stadium thought.

Yankees manager Billy Martin protested to the umpires that Brett had used an illegal bat because it had too much pine tar. (Pine tar is a sticky brown substance batters apply to their bats to give them a better grip.) Baseball rule 1.10 (b) allows a player's bat to have eighteen inches of tar from the end of the bat handle.

"I was feeling pretty good about myself after hitting the homer," Brett recalled. "I was sitting in the dugout. Somebody said they were checking the pine tar, and I said, 'If they call me out for using too much pine tar, I'm going to kill one of those SOBs.'"

The umpires didn't have a ruler to measure the pine tar on Brett's bat, so they placed the lumber across home plate, which measures seventeen inches across. When they did, they saw that the pine tar exceeded the legal limit. The four umpires huddled up again, and then home plate umpire Tim McClelland signaled that Brett was out, meaning his potential game-winning home run was nullified. The game was over; a 4-3 Yankees win.

"I couldn't believe it," said Brett.

"I can sympathize with George," Gossage remarked after the game, "but not that much."

An enraged Brett sprang from the dugout, his eyes bulging like a madman, and he was screaming obscenities as he raced toward McClelland. Umpiring crew chief Joe Brinkman intercepted Brett before he reached McClelland, grabbing him around the neck and trying to calm him down. "In that situation," said Brinkman, "you know something's going to happen. It was quite traumatic. He was upset."

Royals manager Dick Howser joined the skirmish, and was ejected from the game along with Brett. "It knocks you to your knees," said Howser. "I'm sick about it. I don't like it. I don't like it at all. I don't expect my players to accept it."

Meanwhile, Royals pitcher Gaylord Perry, who had long admitted throwing an illegal spitball, grabbed the bat from McClellan and was halfway up the tunnel toward the team locker room to hide the evidence when stadium security personnel grabbed him and grabbed the bat. The bat was given to Brinkman and presumably went on its way to the American League office for inspection.

"I didn't know what was going on," said Howser. "I saw guys in sport coats and ties trying to inter-

Kansas City's George Brett was at the center of one of the most unlikely baseball finishes in Yankees history. (Courtesy of Missouri State Archives via Wikimedia Commons.)

cept the bat. It was like a Brink's robbery. Who's got the gold? Our players had it; the umpires had it. I don't know who has it—the CIA, a think tank at the Pentagon."

The Yankees had won the game by a score of 4 to 3—or so everyone who left the stadium had thought. But the Royals protested the umpire's decision, arguing that Brett had no intentional plan to cheat and that he therefore did not violate the spirit of the rules.

Four days later, American League president Lee MacPhail upheld the Royals' protest. Acknowledging that Brett had pine tar too high on the bat, MacPhail explained it was the league's belief that "games should be won and lost on the playing field, not through technicalities of the rules." MacPhail overruled the umpires' decision, overturning the events on the field, and reinstated the outcome of Brett's at bat, putting the Royals back in front, 5-4. The contest was then declared "suspended."

Following this incident baseball's rulebook was amended to prevent a similar situation from occurring again. The rule now states that the protest must occur before the bat is used in play.

Part Four

Yankees owner George Steinbrenner was miffed. "I wouldn't want to be Lee MacPhail living in New York!" he snapped.

Twenty-five days after it began, on August 18 (an open date for both teams), the "Pine Tar Game" resumed at Yankee Stadium in front of only 1,245 fans. To show their annoyance and mock the proceedings, the Yankees for the final out of the top of the ninth inning played pitcher Ron Guidry in centerfield and first baseman Don Mattingly (a left-handed fielder) at second base. Guidry played center field because the Yankees had traded away Jerry Mumphrey, who had come into the game for defensive purposes. When the game resumed, in protest of the protest, Martin appealed at both first base and second base, claiming Brett had missed touching the bags on his home run trot around the bases. Then New York's George Frazier struck out Hal McRae for the third out of the inning. In the bottom of the ninth, Royals' reliever Dan Quisenberry was able to retire Mattingly, Roy Smalley, and Oscar Gamble in order, and the Royals won by the same 5-4 score.

When Brett was elected to the Baseball Hall of Fame in 1999, the famous pine tar bat went to Cooperstown with him, where it was placed on display.

RAGS' RICHES

Yankee Stadium was buzzing weeks before the infamous Pine Tar Game in 1983, thanks to a no-hitter thrown by New York's Dave Righetti on July 4th against the Boston Red Sox. It was the first no-hitter thrown by a Yankee pitcher since Don Larsen's perfect game in the 1956 World Series. Nobody knew it at the time, but the no-hitter was Righetti's last hurrah as a starting pitcher.

Acquired from the Texas Rangers as part of the Sparky Lyle trade after the 1978 season, Righetti began his Yankees career as a starter and was the 1981 AL Rookie of the Year with an 8-4 record and 2.05 earned run average. In the postseason, he won two games against the Milwaukee Brewers in the divisional series and one game against the Oakland Athletics in the League Championship Series. He won 11 games in 1982 and 14 in 1983, including his no-hitter against Boston.

Moved to the bullpen the next year to replace Rich Gossage as the team's closer, "Rags" made a smooth transition to relief pitching, and went on to average 32 saves over the next seven seasons. Righetti set the major league single-season saves record with 46 in 1986. That season, Righetti converted 29 of his final 30 save chances, including saving both ends of a season-ending doubleheader against the Boston Red Sox at Fenway Park, to break the record of 45 held by Dan Quisenberry and Bruce Sutter. The record would stand until Bobby Thigpen saved 57 games for the Chicago White Sox in 1990.

A two-time All-Star, Righetti has 224 career saves as a Yankee. He also pitched for the San Francisco Giants, Oakland Athletics, Toronto Blue Jays, and Chicago White Sox before retiring in 1995. He has served as the Giants' pitching coach since 2000.

1987

Donnie Baseball

It was a hot summer night in Arlington, Texas, on July 18, 1987, when Don Mattingly, a hard-hitting doubles machine not known for his home run stroke, put his name in the major league baseball record books by belting a home run in an eighth consecutive game. Mattingly's home run hot streak equaled a thirty-one-year-old record many said would never be broken.

The sellout crowd of 41,871 Texas fans—a majority there to see if Mattingly would make history—sat on the edge of their seats when Mattingly came to bat in the first inning at Arlington Stadium. Mattingly's amazing home run streak started July 8, 1987, against Mike Smithson of the Minnesota Twins. Then the Yankees' first baseman also went deep off Minnesota's Juan Berenguer, Chicago's Richard Dotson, Joel McKeon, Jose DeLeon and Jim Winn, and Texas' Charlie Hough, Mitch Williams, and Paul Kilgus.

That set the stage for Mattingly to try to equal the record against Texas' right-hander Juan Guzman. Only one major leaguer, Pittsburgh's Dale Long, another first baseman, had hit homers in eight straight games, back in 1956. (Seattle's Ken Griffey duplicated the record in 1993.) In the fourth inning, Mattingly let Guzman's first two pitches go by for balls. Then on the third pitch he took a mighty swing and connected with the pitch, depositing the ball over the left field fence, just past the outstretched glove of outfielder Ruben Sierra. The roaring fans erupted to give Mattingly a standing ovation as he rounded the bases. The home run was his record tenth during the eight-game span, and his simultaneous streak of 10 games with at least one extra base hit surpassed the American League record set by Babe Ruth in 1921.

The next night, on July 20, Mattingly was held homerless, but in that game he tied the major league record of 22 putouts by a first baseman in a game. During his remarkable 1987 season, Mattingly also hit six grand slam home runs to set a new single-season mark. The record-setting sixth grand slam was hit off Boston's Bruce Hurst, on September 29, 1987. (Cleveland's Travis Hafner tied the mark in 2006.)

During his fourteen seasons in the Bronx, Mattingly grew to be one of the most popular and well-respected Yankees in team history. He showed promise from the start, winning the batting title with a .343 average in his first full season of 1984. He was the American League Most Valuable Player in 1985, when he hit .324 with 35 home runs and 145 runs batted in. The Indiana native with the flowing long hair and rock-star mustache kept getting better. In 1986, he set Yankees records for doubles (53) and hits (238), becoming the first Yankee since Lou Gehrig to collect at least 200 hits for three seasons in a row.

Mattingly matched his hitting with outstanding defense, and won nine Gold Glove awards for his fielding excellence at first base. "Donnie Baseball" put up Hall of Fame-caliber numbers at the plate when healthy. He

Don Mattingly hitting against the Seattle Mariners, August 19, 1988. (RickDikeman via Wikimedia Commons)

had a lifetime batting average of .307 with 222 home runs and 1,099 RBI in a career hampered by a painful back. In 1991, the Yankees appointed Mattingly as the tenth captain in team history. When the aching back was more than he could bear, Mattingly retired after the 1995 playoff series loss to Seattle, a rare Yankees legend to have never reached the World Series. In 1997, his jersey uniform No. 23 was retired and a bronze plaque unveiled, the last line reading: "A Yankee forever."

Part Four

HOMER HEROICS

Don Mattingly may not make it to the Baseball Hall of Fame like Babe Ruth, Lou Gehrig, Joe DiMaggio, and Mickey Mantle, but during the 1987 season, by hitting 10 home runs in 8 games, he accomplished his own home run heroics to overshadow even those Yankees legends. Here is a list of Mattingly's home run binge and the victims he took deep.

Game	Date	Opponent	Pitcher	Inning	Type
1	July 8	Twins	Mike Smithson	1st	3-run
1	July 8	Twins	Juan Berenguer	6th	Solo
2	July 9	White Sox	Richard Dotson	6th	Solo
3	July 10	White Sox	Joel McKeon	2nd	Grand Slam
4	July 11	White Sox	Jose DeLeon	3rd	Solo
5	July 12	White Sox	Jim Winn	7th	Solo
6	July 16	Rangers	Charlie Hough	2nd	Grand Slam
6	July 16	Rangers	Mitch Williams	8th	2-run
7	July 17	Rangers	Paul Kilgus	6th	Solo
8	July 18	Rangers	Jose Guzman	4th	Solo

1993

Inspiration Personified

Since St. Louis Brown Stockings' right-hander George Bradley became the first major league baseball pitcher to do it, on July 15, 1876, pitching a no-hit baseball game has remained a remarkable personal achievement. But as hard as it is to pitch a complete game while allowing no hits, they're not all that uncommon. At least one no-hitter has been thrown in all but five major league seasons (1982, 1985, 1989, 2000, and 2005) since 1960. But the no-hitter pitched on September 4, 1993, at Yankee Stadium by New York Yankees lefthander Jim Abbott is the only one of its kind.

It's not because Abbott struck out only three hitters during the 2-0 victory. Or because he shut down an explosive Cleveland Indians' lineup, featuring such All-Star hitters as Kenny Lofton, Albert Belle, Manny Ramirez, and Jim Thome—who just six days earlier in Cleveland had pounded Abbott for seven runs and knocked him out of the game in the fourth inning. It's because Jim Abbott has only one hand.

His entire life, Abbott has said "no" to accepting pity or being treated differently because he was born without a right hand. And he wouldn't take no for an answer when challenged to prove he belonged on the pitcher's mound. At age eleven, in his Little League pitching debut, he threw a no-hitter. He pitched the gold-medal-winning game for the United States against Japan in the 1988 Summer Olympic Games, in Seoul, South Korea. And without a day in the minor leagues, he jumped directly from the University of Michigan—where he won the Golden Spikes Award as the nation's most outstanding college baseball player—to the California Angels' starting rotation.

"I don't think I'm handicapped," says Abbott. "My hand hasn't kept me from doing anything I wanted to do. I believe you can do anything you want, if you put your mind to it."

Against the Indians, Abbott did not get off to a good start when he issued a leadoff walk to Lofton. But Felix Fermin grounded into a double play and then Abbott settled down. Though Abbott walked five batters, the Indians never advanced a runner past first

Jim Abbott, left, celebrates his no-hit victory over the Cleveland Indians as Wade Boggs runs to congratulate him in New York, September 4, 1993. Boggs had made a key play in the seventh inning to preserve Abbott's no-hitter. (AP Photo/Bebeto Matthews)

base and hit only six balls out of the infield. While recording 15 outs by ground balls, Abbott was assisted by several fine defensive plays from his infielders, most notably by third baseman Wade Boggs, who in the seventh inning dove to his left to snare a bouncer and throw out Belle.

Earlier in the season, Abbott had carried a no-hitter into the eighth inning against the Chicago White Sox, but it was broken up by Bo Jackson's single. This time, however, Abbott would make history. Said first baseman Don Mattingly: "The last couple of innings, I had these huge goose bumps on my forearms, and the hair on the back of my neck was standing up. Maybe that would have happened with someone else. Maybe I'd have the same feelings. But I think because it was Jim there was a little something extra."

Leading off the ninth inning was Lofton, who attempted to force the Yankees' one-handed pitcher to field a bunt, but fouled his attempt off and heard raucous boos from the Stadium crowd before grounding out. Then Fermin smashed a long drive to left centerfield, some 390 feet away, but the ball had enough airtime to allow centerfielder Bernie Williams to run it down. Finally, Carlos Baerga, a switch-hitter, took the unorthodox approach of batting left-handed against the left-handed throwing Abbott, in the hopes of neutralizing Abbott's cut fastball, but the ploy did not work. Baerga hit one last grounder, to shortstop Randy Velarde. When Velarde's throw reached Mattingly's mitt, Abbott exulted. He threw open his arms and shouted, "How about that!" as jubilant teammates mobbed him near the mound. It was the first no-hitter at Yankee Stadium since Dave Righetti did it ten years earlier.

The normally stoic Yankees manager Buck Showalter jumped off the bench in celebration and nearly banged his head on the dugout roof. The last out provided him with welcome relief. "No one wants to be blamed for doing anything to jinx a no-hitter," said Showalter. "I had to go to the bathroom for the last four innings, but I was afraid to go."

The next morning, the Yankee Stadium grounds crew, which had dug out the pitching rubber from the mound, presented Abbott with the slab, which all of his teammates had signed. The Hall of Fame called for his hat and the baseball.

"The pitching rubber [is] very heavy. It weighs about 25 pounds," says Abbott. "I have it right outside my office at home. It's a great piece of memorabilia."

Part Four

THE NO-NOS

Yankees pitchers have hurled eleven no-hitters, including three perfect games. Monte Pearson pitched the first no-hitter in Yankee Stadium history, in the second game of a doubleheader against the Cleveland Indians on August 27, 1938.

No-Hitters Thrown by Yankee Pitchers			
Pitcher	Opponent	Date	Score
George Mogridge	@ Boston	4/24/1917	2-1
Sad Sam Jones	@ Philadelphia	9/4/1923	2-0
Monte Pearson	Cleveland	8/27/1938	13-0
Allie Reynolds	@ Cleveland	7/12/1951	1-0
Allie Reynolds	Boston	9/28/1951	8-0
Don Larsen*	Brooklyn	10/8/1956	2-0
Dave Righetti	Boston	7/4/1983	4-0
Jim Abbott	Cleveland	9/4/1993	4-0
Dwight Gooden	Seattle	5/14/1996	2-0
David Wells*	Minnesota	5/17/1998	4-0
David Cone*	Montreal	7/18/1999	6-0

(*Designates a perfect game.)

PART FIVE

THE CORE FOUR

Derek Jeter had a Rookie of the Year season in 1996 and went on the become the face of the Yankees for the better part of two decades. (Keith Allison via Wikimedia Commons)

1996

A New Dynasty Emerges

In 1995, the Yankees, managed by Buck Showalter, finished with a record of 79-65, qualifying for the postseason as the first American League wild card team under the new postseason rules. In the playoffs against the Mariners they jumped out a to 2-0 series lead, but then lost three heartbreaking games in a row. When Ken Griffey Jr. slid across home plate to score the clinching run for Seattle, ending the hopeful Yankees 1995 season, it put into motion a series of events that would set the stage for a new Yankees dynasty.

When the Yankees hired Joe Torre as manager prior to the 1996 season, the *New York Daily News* dubbed Torre "Clueless Joe" with a back page headline that lives in baseball infamy. At the time, though, few could have predicted the overwhelming and enormous success to come. Due to a combination of his charismatic personality, his knowledge of the game having played it, and the moxie to stand up to Yankees owner George Steinbrenner, Torre became a beloved figure during his twelve years as the skipper of baseball's most successful franchise.

The 1996 team was an eclectic mix of homegrown stars and hired guns. Of the twenty-five players on the Yankees' 1996 roster, only nine had been on the roster against the Mariners a year earlier. Pitcher David Cone, acquired by the Yankees in a trade during the 1995 season, was re-signed as a free agent following the season. Tino Martinez was traded to the team before the season, replacing legendary first baseman Don Mattingly. Joe Girardi signed with the Yankees before the season and was their starting catcher. Andy Pettitte was in his second season but had arguably the best year of his career, winning 21 games and finishing second in the Cy Young award voting. And perhaps most notably, Derek Jeter, in his first full season as shortstop with the Yankees, hit .314 and won the Rookie of the Year award.

The new-look Yankees won 92 games in 1996, finishing atop the American League East Division for the first time since 1981. In the divisional playoff round the Yankees

141

defeated the Texas Rangers in four games, thanks to New York's shutdown relief pitching. The Yankees' bullpen recorded wins in Games 2, 3 and 4, allowing just one earned run in 20 innings during the series.

The late-inning heroics continued during the American League Championship Series against the Baltimore Orioles. In the eighth inning of the first game, with the Yankees trailing 4-3, Jeffrey Maier, a twelve-year-old fan, reached over the right-field wall and deflected a Derek Jeter fly ball into the stands. The umpires ruled it a home run that tied the score. The Yankees went on to win, 5-4, when Bernie Williams smacked a walk-off homer off Randy Myers in the 11th inning.

Orioles' right fielder Tony Tarasco stretches for the ball as young Yankee fan Jeff Maier deflects it during Game 1 of the American League Championship Series against the Yankees on October 9, 1996. (AP Photo/Mark Lennihan, File)

Williams hit .474 and was the series Most Valuable Player, but it was Darryl Strawberry who had the best postseason series of his career. In the Yankees' five-game triumph over the Orioles, Strawberry hit .417 (5 for 12) with three home runs. Two of those homers came in Game 4, an 8-4 Yankees victory that put them on the brink of their first AL championship in fifteen years. Strawberry's second homer, a two-run shot in the eighth inning off Armando Benitez, provided the Yankees with important insurance runs before John Wetteland closed it out in the ninth. The next day, Strawberry showed that he was not finished, and hit a home run to help the Yankees close out the series with a 6-4 victory.

Bernie Williams was the MVP of the 1996 ALCS and a beloved Yankee for sixteen seasons. (clare_and_ben via Wikimedia Commons)

The Yankees were returning to the Fall Classic for the first time since losing to the Los Angeles Dodgers in 1981. It had been 18 years since the Yankees had won a World Series. Their longest previous dry spell since winning their first title in 1923 had been from 1962 to 1977. And it looked for a while like the 1996 title would go to the defending champion Atlanta Braves, a team with the most imposing pitching staff in baseball. John Smoltz was an easy winner over Andy Pettitte in the opener, 12-1, at Yankee Stadium. Adding insult to embarrassment for the Yankees, the Braves' 19-year-old Andruw Jones broke Mickey Mantle's record by becoming the youngest player ever to hit a World Series home run. In fact, he hit two in the game.

Greg Maddux, the four-time Cy Young Award winner, was masterful in Game 2, blanking the Yankees on six hits over eight innings. After dropping the first two games of the series by a combined score of 16-1, Torre famously calmed down a furious Steinbrenner by assuring him that the team would win three straight in Atlanta before finishing the series in six games. "I told George that . . . there was nothing to worry about. We would go down to Atlanta and take care of business because Atlanta was my town. He looked at me like I was crazy, but he didn't say anything else." One week later, Torre's prediction came to pass.

In World Series history, only two teams had ever come back to win after dropping the first two games at home. "I don't know any words of wisdom when you go down 0-2 against the defending world champions," said David Cone, New York's Game 3 starter. The Yankees did not need wisdom, they needed some clutch hits and good pitching, and they got both to back Cone's 5-2 win. The Yankees, trailing two games to one in the World Series and 6-0 after five innings, then rallied to stun the Braves, 8-6, in 10 innings, at Atlanta. After three runs in the sixth, the Bombers tied it on Jim Leyritz's three-run homer in the eighth, and won it on Wade Boggs' bases-loaded, two-out walk.

After the dramatic Game 4 win, Pettitte kept the Yankee momentum going by out-dueling Smoltz the next night, pitching a five-hit, 1-0 shutout against the Braves going into the ninth inning. Torre then brought relief ace John Wetteland in to preserve the victory. With Braves on first and third and two outs, Luis Polonia stood in the batter's box at Fulton County Stadium and fouled off six Wetteland fastballs before connecting and sending a searing line drive into right center field. The right fielder, Paul O'Neill, playing despite a painful left hamstring, ran with a hobbled gait toward the ball that looked like it was going to win the game for the Braves. But at the last instant O'Neill lunged and snared the ball for the final out and saved the game.

"I'm glad I had enough to get to the ball," he said.

So were a lot of Yankees fans. Two nights later, catcher Joe Girardi's triple in the third inning of Game 6 drove in a run, and he later scored from third. The Yankees' three-run rally that inning was all Jimmy Key needed to defeat Maddux, 3-2, in the title-clinching game. "They [the Braves] said they could beat the '27 Yankees. But they forgot about the '96 Yankees," said Girardi.

The Yanks were champs for the first time since 1978. The triumph started a run of four Yankee titles in five years. John Wetteland saved each of the Yankees' victories, earning the series most valuable player honors. Third baseman Boggs, who during the regular season had hit over .300 for the fourteenth time in his Hall of Fame career, celebrated by trotting around Yankee Stadium on the back of a policeman's horse.

THE KING OF CLUTCH

Jim Leyritz was known for his brash playing style, irritating opponents with his bat twirling at the plate, and teammates with his cock-sure swagger, earning him the nickname "The King." But when the journeyman catcher was in the lineup, especially in the postseason, he always made the best of his opportunities, hitting home runs when it mattered most. In fact, eight of Leyritz's thirteen postseason hits were home runs, and many of them were the turning point of the series.

Leyritz first made his mark in the 1995 Division Series against the Seattle Mariners. In Game 2 at Yankee Stadium, Leyritz hit a two-run home run in the rain off Seattle pitcher Tim Belcher into the right-centerfield bleachers in the 15th inning to win the game 7-5. The Yankees, who hadn't won anything since 1981, took a commanding two-game lead in the best-of-five series. Unable to close out the series, New York lost the next three games in Seattle's Kingdome, and the Mariners, in the postseason for the first time in team history, won a thrilling, extra-innings victory in game five of the division series.

The most famous of Leyritz's playoff heroics occurred in Game 4 of the 1996 World Series against the Atlanta Braves at Fulton County Stadium in Atlanta. The Yankees had lost the first two games of the series at home, and narrowly won Game 3 in Atlanta. The Braves had built a 6-0 lead through five innings and seem poised to take a 3-1 lead in the World Series. Leyritz entered the game for catcher Joe Girardi in the sixth inning after New York had rallied for three runs to cut the deficit to 6-3. In the eighth, Braves manager Bobby Cox brought in closer Mark Wohlers to finish the job for the Braves. Wohlers had saved 39 games for Atlanta during the regular season and his fastball regularly hit 100 miles per hour on the radar gun. After two runners reached base, Leyritz stepped into the batter's box with one out. He worked the count to 2-2, fouling off two wicked fastballs. Then Wohlers threw a hanging slider and Leyritz jumped all over it, lacing a high-arcing fly ball that soared over the left-field fence for a three-run homer to tie the game and swing the momentum in the Yankees' favor.

"I'm not thinking home run right there," said Leyritz. "I'm thinking I've got an opportunity to drive in one run if I get a base hit."

The Yankees would go on to win 8-6 in 10 innings to tie the Series at two games apiece, and they won it in six games. Leyritz's dramatic home run remains the signature moment of that series and of his career. It was also the turning point of the franchise. With one swing of the bat, Leyritz ignited a new Yankees dynasty, starting a run of four titles in five years.

"You win that game or else it is 3-to-1," said Yankees manager Joe Torre. "Instead, you had the snowball effect and win that year and it makes you feel different and able to win after that, no question. Leyritz's homer was huge. You know, Jimmy blew his own horn on how many big hits he had, but, you know what, Jimmy had a lot of big hits."

Despite his big-game success, Leyritz was traded four times over the next two years. Playing with the San Diego Padres in the 1998 division series against Houston he hit three homers, including a two-out, game-tying homer in the ninth inning of Game 2. For good measure, he added another homer in the league championship series victory over Atlanta, a team surely sick of seeing Leyritz step up the plate in big spots.

Traded back to New York in 1999, just in time for the World Series, also against the Atlanta Braves, Leyritz made a pinch-hitting appearance in the eighth inning of Game 4 with the Yankees leading 3-1. Leyritz hammered a solo homer to extend the Yankees lead to 4-1. The Yankees won the game and the series four games to none. Leyritz's shot turned out to be the last major-league home run hit in the 20th century.

1998

Boomer's Big Day

Twenty-seven batters come to the plate. Twenty-seven batters make out. No runner reaches base for any reason in any inning. It's a perfect game, one of the most difficult feats in sports and a baseball pitching rarity.

On May 17, 1998, at Yankee Stadium, portly veteran left-hander David Wells pitched only the 15th perfect game in major league baseball history, retiring all 27 Minnesota Twins he faced in a 4-0 Yankees victory. Relying on pinpoint control of his fastball and curve, Wells was in total command on the mound. No Twins batter could touch him. Wells struck out 11 of the 27 Twins he faced, including Ron Coomer, Jon Shave, and Javier Valentin twice.

Renowned for his excess weight and excessive ways off the field, for at least one day everyone focused on Wells' pitching excellence. "Nobody can ever take this away from me, ever, no matter what," said Wells.

Hours earlier, Wells felt far less elated. He said he was out until five o'clock in the morning, and that he arrived at his stadium locker in sorry shape. Then he found a quiet area in the player's lounge, where he drank half a pot of strong coffee and gulped a handful of aspirin. By game time, Wells had recovered well enough to begin stringing together innings of three up and three down. When he got into the seventh inning, Wells may have been tiring. He got behind in the count on eight of the last nine batters he faced, including Paul Molitor, a member of the 3,000-hit club and a Hall of Famer, who ran the count to 3-and-1 before fanning. The excited Yankee Stadium crowd exhaled in relief.

One of baseball's time-honored superstitions forbids a teammate to talk to a pitcher in the middle of his no-hitter for fear of jinxing him. Yet Wells, always one to buck tradition, was the one hoping to make conversation with someone in the dugout. "I just wanted to talk so it would ease my mind a little bit, but no one would come near me," Wells said later. Finally, pitcher David Cone joked that Wells should start throwing a new pitch.

"Coney comes over to me before the eighth inning and says, 'Guess it's time to break out your knuckleball,'" said Wells.

Cone kept Wells relaxed, and Yankees second baseman Knoblauch would keep him perfect, robbing Coomer of the only potential hit with a slick backhanded stab of a hard one-hop smash near second base in the eighth inning. It would be Wells's biggest scare.

David Wells is carried off the field after pitching a perfect game against the Minnesota Twins Sunday, May 17, 1998 at Yankee Stadium. Wells struck out 11 batters in the Yankees 4-0 victory. (AP Photo/John Dunn)

As he took the mound for the ninth inning, the crowd of 49,820 greeted Wells with a standing ovation. He continued his mastery, inducing a lazy fly ball from Shave and striking out Valentin.

"The fans were going crazy, which was great, but I kind of wanted them to calm down because they were making me nervous," Wells said. "By the end I could barely grip the ball, my hand was shaking so much."

Then the Boomer, as he's known, took a deep breath and threw a fastball to Pat Meares. When Meares's popup landed in right fielder Paul O'Neill's glove for the final out, Wells jumped high in the air, waving his arms in delight, and then embraced his catcher, Jorge Posada, and screamed, "This is great!"

Then the 245-pound Wells was carried off the field by three teammates. He whipped off his cap and waved it at the crowd. To punctuate the historic moment, the voice of Frank Sinatra singing *New York, New York*, which always signals a Yankees victory, filled the stadium. It was a poignant scene, coming just three days after the beloved crooner's death.

After the game Wells fielded a congratulatory call from fellow San Diego native Don Larsen, who had pitched the only other perfect game in Yankees history, against the Brooklyn Dodgers in the 1956 World Series. Coincidentally, both men attended the same high school, Point Loma, in San Diego. Larsen graduated in 1947, Wells was class of 1982.

The next call came from New York City mayor Rudy Giuliani, who invited Wells to city hall to give him a key to the city. To which Wells jokingly replied, "Do you think that's a good idea?"

Hey, David Wells, New York is the city that never sleeps.

1999

Finally Perfect

An early-arriving crowd of 41,930 marched eagerly into Yankee Stadium on July 18, 1999, before a game between the home team Yankees and the Montreal Expos. They had come to the Bronx for Yogi Berra Day to welcome a returning hero. Having been fired as manager in 1985, and then vowing never to enter Yankee Stadium while George Steinbrenner owned the team, Berra had settled his differences with The Boss. After fourteen years of self-imposed exile, the franchise's most beloved catcher was finally coming back to the stadium for a long overdue tribute.

The day was supposed to belong to Berra, who as a player had helped the Yankees win ten World Series championships. Several old-timers including Whitey Ford, Phil Rizzuto, Gil McDougald, and Bobby Richardson, had ventured to the venerable ball park to honor him in a thirty-minute pre-game ceremony. Then Don Larsen threw out the ceremonial first pitch to Berra, who had been Larsen's battery mate in the only World Series perfect game at Yankee Stadium in 1956.

Pitching for the Yankees that day was David Cone, a right-hander with more deliveries than Jay Leno. After Larsen completed his toss, he and Cone shook hands near the mound. Cone jokingly asked if Larsen was going to jump into Yogi's arms like he did in 1956. According to Cone, Larsen said, "Kid, you got it wrong. It was Yogi jumped into my arms."

If Cone made another mistake that afternoon, the Expos batters would have swung and missed. He retired the side in order in the first and second innings. After a 33-minute rain delay, he struck out the side in the third inning, and whizzed through a 1-2-3 fourth. By the sixth inning, the fans at Yankee Stadium were reveling in every pitch, and when Rondell White struck out to end the seventh, the crowd's roar lingered long after Cone had disappeared into the dugout.

The fans in Yankee Stadium were buzzing. Only six outs to go and Cone would accomplish the unthinkable—upstaging Yogi Berra on Yogi Berra Day—by pitching a perfect game. Brad Fullmer whiffed for out No. 24. Three out away. In the ninth, when Orlando Cabrera popped to third baseman Scott Brosius for the final out, Cone dropped to his knees and grabbed his head in disbelief like Bjorn Borg winning Wimbledon. After being carried off the field by his teammates, Cone told reporters: "I probably have a better chance of winning the lottery than this happening today. It makes you stop and think about the Yankee magic and the mystique of this ballpark."

He retired all twenty-seven Montreal batters he faced as the Yankees defeated the Expos, 6-0. It was only the sixteenth perfect game in major league baseball history, and yet the third at Yankee Stadium. (It came only one season after David Wells accomplished the feat.) Of the previous fifteen perfect games, Cone's was perhaps the most efficient. He threw only 88 pitches—an average of less than 10 pitches per inning—and didn't go to a

Less than a year after David Wells pitched a perfect game for the Yankees, David Cone threw another one on Yogi Berra Day at Yankee Stadium. (clare_and_ben via Wikimedia Commons)

three-ball count on a single batter. Working in stifling 95-degree heat, Cone was coolly in command; he used a wicked slider to strike out 10, induce 13 fly outs, and four grounders. His premier performance was all the more remarkable because of his age—at thirty-six he became the oldest pitcher to throw a perfect game since Cy Young in 1904—and the career-threatening surgery he endured three seasons earlier. Doctors discovered an aneurysm in Cone's pitching arm in 1996. In his first game back from surgery he flirted with a no-hitter for seven innings against the Oakland Athletics before being relieved to protect the surgically repaired shoulder.

Cone, who pitched three career one-hitters, said he wondered if he'd ever get a chance at a no-hitter again. "Going into the latter innings today, running through my mind [was] how many times I've been close and how this might be the last chance I get," he said. "My heart was pumping. I could feel it through my uniform."

One man in the stands could identify with what Cone was feeling. "I was just thinking about my day," said Larsen. "I'm sure David will think about this every day of his life."

As Yogi would say, it's déjà vu all over again.

1999

Yankees Sweep Again

The Yankees, though not quite perfect, came pretty darn close in 1998. With an ideal combination of outstanding pitching, timely hitting, solid defense, and unselfish team chemistry, the Yankees won an American League record 114 games in the regular season (against just 48 losses). After sweeping the Texas Rangers in the best-of-five-games divisional playoffs, the Yankees found themselves in trouble against the Cleveland Indians in the American League Championship Series. The Yankees won the opener, 7-2, but lost Game 2 in twelve innings when Chuck Knoblauch failed to call time when arguing a play at first base. In the third game, Cleveland socked four homers and got a complete game from Bartolo Colon.

To avoid an early exit from the playoffs after compiling the best record in team history (114-48), the Yankees needed a big performance in Game 4 in Cleveland and got one from Orlando "El Duque" Hernandez. Hernandez delivered by striking out six batters in seven innings as he combined with Mike Stanton and Mariano Rivera on a four-hit shutout. The Yankees won again the next day and wrapped up the series in six games at Yankee Stadium.

Tino Martinez belted a grand slam in Game 1 of the 1998 World Series to highlight a seven-run seventh inning for the Yankees, who knocked the San Diego Padres on their heels with a come-from-behind triumph. Trailing 5-2, the Yankees had tied the game earlier in the inning on Chuck Knoblauch's three-run homer. The Yankees then loaded the bases, and left-handed pitcher Mark Langston, brought in to face O'Neill after Jeter singled following Knoblauch's homer, now faced the lefty-swinging Martinez. With the count at 2-2, Martinez let pass a very close pitch, which the umpire called ball three. Then, on the 3-2 pitch, Martinez hit a grand slam into the upper deck at Yankee Stadium, giving the Yankees a four-run lead. New York went on to sweep the series and begin a streak of three world titles in a row.

According to Derek Jeter, "Tino's always been one of the fan favorites. One thing about these fans is they don't forget." Along with Martinez's solid defense and clutch hitting, fans have never forgotten his grand slam in Game 1 of the 1998 World Series, that's for sure. (clare_and_ ben via Wikimedia Commons)

In 1999, after winning the American League East division title with 98 wins, the Yankees powered through two rounds of the playoffs to meet the Atlanta Braves again in the World Series. It was billed as a showdown to decide not just the best team of the year, but also the best team of the decade. Although the Braves had only captured one World Series since 1990 (defeating the Cleveland Indians in 1997), compared to two World Series titles for the Yankees (against Atlanta in 1996 and San Diego in 1998), the Braves had dominated the National League, winning eight division titles and five league championships.

It didn't turn out to be much of a battle. But for the lone defeat against eventual AL Cy Young Award winner Pedro Martinez of the Boston Red Sox in game three of the league championship series, the Yankees went undefeated in the postseason, winning 11 of

12 games. In sweeping the Braves in four straight games, the Yankees starting pitchers only gave up seven earned runs and held opposing batters to a paltry .200 average. New York relief pitcher and Series MVP Mariano Rivera pitched 4 2/3 innings, earned two saves, and registered an unblemished earned run average of 0.00. Said Joe Torre, "He's (Mariano Rivera) the best I've ever been around. Not only the ability to pitch and perform under pressure, but the calm he puts over the clubhouse. He's very important for us because he's a special person."

Mariano Rivera was the 1999 World Series MVP. (Keith Allison via Wikimedia Commons)

CURTIS'S BAT SAYS IT ALL

In his only start of the 1999 World Series, Chad Curtis made an impact. He smashed two home runs to bring the Yankees back from a 5-1 deficit in Game 3, including the game-winner in the 10th inning for a dramatic 6-5 victory over Atlanta. The Yankees went on to sweep the Braves in four straight games.

Curtis's homer over the left-centerfield fence off lefty relief specialist Mike Remlinger was the first walk-off World Series homer since Joe Carter in Game 6 in 1993. It was also the first game-ending homer by a Yankee in the World Series since Mickey Mantle slugged one against the St. Louis Cardinals in Game 3 in 1964.

This might be the only time that Curtis, a journeyman outfielder with a .264 lifetime batting average over a 10-year career, is linked with one of the premier players in baseball history, but that is why it was such a memorable night.

"It was a rush," Curtis said. "I can't say I ever felt that before. Rounding the bases, I was kind of tingling. I've heard people talk about that, but I've never felt it before. I was tingling."

After the game, Curtis refused to answer a question posed by sportscaster Jim Gray. Curtis felt, as did most players, that Gray's interview of Pete Rose prior to Game 2 had been too aggressive.

2000

Subway Series

After the Yankees limped to the finish line in 2000 with 87 victories, the club returned
to its predictable postseason pattern. In the league championship series against the Seattle
Mariners, David Justice helped get the Yankees to their third straight World Series with a
three-run home run in Game 6 off lefty reliever Arthur Rhodes. The blast into the upper
deck in right field put the Yankees up 6-4 and sent them on their way to a 9-7 clinching
victory.

With the Mets having defeated the Cardinals in the National League championship
series, the 2000 World Series was New York's first Subway Series in forty-four years—and
the first between the Yankees and Mets. Todd Zeile's drive in the sixth inning of Game 1
at Yankee Stadium bounced off the top of the wall. David Justice picked it up, fired it to
Derek Jeter and Jeter relayed the ball to Jorge Posada, who tagged Timo Perez to end the
top of the sixth inning with the game still scoreless. The Yankees got two runs in the bottom of the inning, but the Mets took the lead in the top of the seventh. In the ninth, Paul
O'Neill drew a hard-fought walk from Mets closer Armando Benitez and came around to
score the tying run on a sacrifice fly. After the Yankees squandered golden opportunities
to score in the tenth and eleventh, former Met Jose Vizcaino finally ended the game with
a bases loaded single in the twelfth.

The Yankees won again the next night, 6-5, holding on in the ninth inning after brilliant pitching from Roger Clemens, who overshadowed his own performance by flinging
a piece of a broken bat at Mets slugger Mike Piazza in the first inning. The win marked
the team's fourteenth consecutive victory in World Series play, breaking the twelve-game
record of the 1927, 1928, and 1932 Yankees. In the Game 5 clincher at Shea Stadium,
Andy Pettitte and the Mets' Al Leiter staged a marvelous pitching duel. With the score tied
2-2 in the ninth, Leiter finally ran out of steam when Luis Sojo, a Yankee reserve, clubbed
the biggest single of his life that scored the winning run. Piazza later lined out to Bernie

Roger Clemens fields Mike Piazza's broken bat in the first inning of Game 2 of the 2000 World Series at Yankee Stadium. (AP Photo/Ron Frehm)

Williams in center in the bottom of the inning to end it. The Yankees won their third consecutive world championship, 26th overall title, and became the first club to win three straight World Series since the 1972-74 Oakland Athletics.

YANKEES IN THE SUBWAY SERIES

There have been twelve championship Subway Series and the Yankees, as the only American League team based in New York, have appeared in all of them, compiling a dominant 11-1 all-time Subway Series record.

- 1923—Yankees 4, Giants 2

Casey Stengel hit two home runs to win two games for the Giants, but Babe Ruth swatted three solo home runs and Herb Pennock won two games to help the Yankees open Yankee Stadium in grand style with the first of their 27 world championships.

- 1936—Yankees 4, Giants 2

The Yankees offense explodes, scoring 18 runs in Game 2 and 13 runs in the clinching Game 6. Lou Gehrig hits two home runs and drives in seven runs, rookie Joe DiMaggio hits .346, and Red Rolfe has 10 hits.

- 1937—Yankees 4, Giants 1

The Yankees take the first two games by identical 8-1 scores. Lefty Gomez wins two games and drives in the go-ahead run in Game 5 to win the clincher for a second straight year.

- 1941—Yankees 4, Dodgers 1

Tiny Bonham, Red Ruffing and Marius Russo each pitch complete games and Mickey Owen's dropped third strike on Tommy Henrich in Game 4 dooms the Dodgers.

- 1947—Yankees 4, Dodgers 3

Yankees win a memorable series despite Cookie Lavagetto spoiling Bill Bevens' no-hit bid in the ninth inning of Game 4 and Al Gionfriddo's homer-robbing catch of Joe DiMaggio's long drive in Game 6.

- 1949—Yankees 4, Dodgers 1

On the final day of the season, Tommy Henrich's leadoff eighth-inning home run gives the Yankees a 2-0 lead and propels the Bombers to a 5-3 win over the Red Sox in front of 68,055 roaring fans at the Stadium. The win gives the Yanks the American League pennant by one game over Boston and first-year manager Casey Stengel the first of his 10 pennants. Henrich continued his hot hitting in the World Series against the Dodgers; his Game 1 home run was all Allie Reynolds needed in a 1-0 Yankees victory.

- 1951—Yankees 4, Giants 2

  In the Game 6 clincher, Hank Bauer's bases-loaded triple with two outs in the sixth inning cleared the bases to give the Yankees a 4-1 lead. Then, in the ninth inning, after the Giants closed the deficit to 4-3 and with the tying run in scoring position, a racing Bauer made a sensational catch on a low line drive to end the game.

- 1952—Yankees 4, Dodgers 3

  Brooklyn, still in search of its first championship, had a 3-2 series lead, but couldn't put the Yankees away in the sixth game. In Game 7, Billy Martin makes a game-saving catch of Jackie Robinson's bases-loaded infield popup. The Dodgers lost in the World Series for the sixth time in six tries.

- 1953—Yankees 4, Dodgers 2

  The Yankees added to the Dodgers' frustration by winning the World Series again from their Brooklyn neighbors. New York's six-game victory was its record fifth championship in a row. Billy Martin wins the series for the Yankees in Game 6 with a run-scoring single in the ninth inning.

- 1955—Dodgers 4, Yankees 3

  Jackie Robinson steals home in eighth inning of the series opener. Sandy Amoros makes a game-saving running catch of Yogi Berra's fly ball near the left-field foul pole as Johnny Podres blanks the Yankees 2-0 in Game 7.

- 1956—Yankees 4, Dodgers 3

  In Game 5, Don Larsen pitches the only perfect game and no-hitter in Series history. Johnny Kucks clinches it with a shutout in Game 7.

- 2000—Yankees 4, Mets 1

  Jose Vizcaino singles home the winning run in the 12th inning to take Game 1; Roger Clemens hurls a broken bat at Mike Piazza in Game 2; series MVP Derek Jeter homers to lead off Game 4 at Shea Stadium; and a two-out ninth inning single by Luis Sojo brings in the clinching run in Game 5.

2001

The Flip Play

Game three of the 2001 American League Division Series featured Derek Jeter's most famous highlight reel: his sprint across the field and backhanded flip relay to Jorge Posada which nailed Oakland's Jeremy Giambi at the plate in the seventh inning to preserve the Yankees' 1-0 win.

"It was like Superman flying out of the sky to save the season," said general manager Brian Cashman.

The Yankees, winners of the American League East by 13½ games, entered the post-season as the three-time defending champion and heavy favorite in the American League Division Series against the Oakland Athletics. But the Yankees got off to a rough start, losing the first two games of this best-of-five series in the Bronx. The dynasty looked dead as the Yankees traveled to Oakland with history against them. No team had ever won a best-of-five series after losing the first two games at home.

Now the series had moved to Oakland and the Yankees were in danger of being swept. In the seventh inning of the third game, New York was clinging to a 1-0 lead thanks to catcher Jorge Posada's homer. Mike Mussina was making his first playoff start for the Yankees, but his Oakland counterpart, Barry Zito, had held the Yanks to just two hits, one of which had left the yard for the game's only run. With Oakland's Jeremy Giambi on first base and two outs, Terrence Long ripped Mussina's 100th pitch for a double down the first-base line. As the ball rattled off the wall, Giambi ran around third base heading for home. Though not fleet of foot, Giambi seemed a sure bet to score the tying run.

Outfielder Shane Spencer retrieved the ball in the right-field corner and fired a throw that sailed over the head of the first cut-off man, second baseman Alfonso Soriano, and the second cut-off man, first baseman Tino Martinez. Standing at his infield position, Derek Jeter saw the situation developing and that's when the twenty-seven-year-old shortstop decided to dash across the infield grass and chase down a throw he realized was too high for either Soriano or Martinez to catch. Nobody knows why Jeter was in position to react that way. "It was my job to read the play," Jeter said later.

Jeter caught the ball on a bounce on the first-base line about twenty feet from home plate, running toward the first base dugout and away from Posada. Jeter, with his momentum taking him away from home plate, had the presence of mind to flip the ball to Posada so the catcher would receive it on the third-base side of home plate. For some reason, perhaps expecting a collision, Giambi did not slide—he ran across the plate standing up. Posada caught the ball and slapped a tag on Giambi's right leg a blink of an eye before Giambi's right foot landed on home plate. Umpire Kerwin Danley signaled Giambi out at home. "If he slides," Posada said, "I don't have a chance."

Derek Jeter flips the ball to Jorge Posada who tags out the A's Jeremy Giambi at home to prevent a sweep by Oakland in the 2001 ALDS. The Yanklees would win the series and go on to another World Series. (AP Photo/Eric Risberg, File)

Mariano Rivera held the A's scoreless over the final two innings to secure the game three victory, and the Yankees won again the next day to force a deciding game five in the Bronx. Prior to the game, the Yankees Hall of Fame shortstop Phil Rizzuto followed-up his ceremonial first pitch by pulling a second ball out of his pocket, trotting toward the first-base line, and then flipping the ball back to the catcher in a perfect Jeter imitation.

The Yankee Stadium crowd loved it, but not as much as they love the original. The Yankees were leading 5-3 with one out and Oakland's Eric Chavez on first, Terrence Long, the same batter whose Game 3 double led to Jeter's flip play, lifted a high foul ball behind third base. Jeter chased after it, and reached for the ball far into the stands. Jeter's momentum caused him to flip over the railing spikes-first and crash-land flat on his back against the cement floor of the photographers' pit. The crowd of 56,642 gasped when Jeter disappeared from view, fearing for the shortstop's safety. Jeter suffered only a cut on his elbow, but more important, he had caught the ball. As Jeter climbed back over the railing and onto the field, the fans chanted his name. "It felt good," Jeter said of the chant.

Rivera again pitched the final two scoreless innings, and the Yankees became the first team to lose the first two games of a best-of-five at home and then win the series. Jeter delivered big. He batted .444 in the series and saved the Yankees from near-certain elimination with his instincts in game three.

"We definitely win the series if Jeter doesn't make that flip play," said Oakland's front office executive J.P. Ricciardi.

But Jeter did make that flip play, and it saved the Yankees postseason.

2001

Mystique and Aura

The New York Yankees were trailing the Arizona Diamondbacks two games to none in the 2001 World Series, but they were coming home to the Bronx to play the next three games at Yankee Stadium. After the Yankees won a hard-fought 2-1 victory in Game 3, Curt Schilling, who would be on the Yankee Stadium mound as Arizona's Game 4 starting pitcher, was asked to comment on the mystique and aura of Yankee Stadium, as evidenced by the team's unprecedented championship tradition.

"Mystique and aura," Schilling said of the idea of Yankees magic, "those are dancers in a night club."

He couldn't have been farther off base.

On October 31, 2001, Yankee Stadium hosted the first major league baseball game ever played on Halloween. Appropriately, the game had a bizarre finish. Schilling had stymied the Yankees for seven innings and left the game with a two-run lead. Arizona's side-arming relief pitcher Byung-Hyun Kim entered the game with a charge to record the final six outs. He dispatched the Yankees quickly in the eighth, and with two outs in the ninth inning the Yankees were one out away from going down in the Series three games to one. Paul O'Neill was on first base and Tino Martinez, hitless in his previous 10 plate appearances, was in the batter's box. Kim seemed unhittable, and the Yankees needed a miracle. They got one. On Kim's first pitch, Martinez swung and lashed a high-arcing line drive that carried over the right-center field wall for a dramatic home run to tie the score. The stadium's upper tiers were rocking and the concrete floor was rolling. A fan's poster said it all that night: "We're Back." How true it was. Just weeks after the September 11 tragedy, New Yorkers were counting mightily on the Yankees to help restore the pride and spirit of their indomitable city. And now a critical game so perilously close to being lost had new life.

As the game went into extra innings, the stadium clock struck midnight. It was now November 1—the first time a World Series game was ever played in November.

The Yankees' captain, Derek Jeter, fouled off three tough pitches from the South Korean reliever before running the count full. Then Jeter smacked Kim's next pitch toward the right field corner. The ball snuck inside the foul pole and landed in the first row of seats for a game-winning home run to even the Series at two games apiece. The crowd erupted with a primordial scream lasting several minutes as Jeter trotted around the bases, his right fist raised in the air, before jumping onto home plate and into the waiting arms of his jubilant teammates.

The gravity of the moment was not lost on Jeter.

"I've never hit a walk-off homer," said the Yankees' new Mr. November. "I don't think I hit one in Little League. That was huge."

The next night, in Game 5, Arizona again held a two-run lead in the ninth inning, and once more, manager Bob Brenly called on Kim to protect it. Jorge Posada was on second base with two outs, and the Yankees were again down to their last out, just as they were when Martinez tied Game 4 with a homer off Kim. This time, Scott Brosius played the hero, connecting on Kim's second pitch and propelling the ball deep beyond the left-field wall. It was the second time in as many nights the Yankees had come back from the brink of defeat by hitting a two-run home run with two outs in the ninth to tie the game.

"It's Groundhog Day," said Joe Torre. "This is the most incredible couple of games I've ever managed."

As Brosius began to celebrate his two-run homer, the rampant emotion throughout the Stadium crackled like lightning, and the buzzing didn't stop until the smoke had cleared in the twelfth inning, when Alfonso Soriano singled home Chuck Knoblauch with the winning run for a 3-2 Yankees Series lead.

A fan sitting behind the Arizona dugout unfurled a banner that read: "Mystique and aura appearing nightly." The Yankees had done it again.

Sadly, the magic didn't last. Despite taking a 2-1 lead on an Alfonoso Soriano solo homer in the eighth inning of Game 7, the Yankees allowed two runs in the ninth and lost one of the most thrilling World Series of all time.

PRESIDENTIAL PITCH

The national mourning in the aftermath of the September 11, 2001, terrorist attacks had resulted in the extension of that year's baseball season, so Game 3 of the 2001 World Series, played on October 30, marked the latest date that a major league baseball game had ever been contested.

Moments before game time, a tall right-hander from Texas popped out of the Yankees dugout and began striding toward the pitcher's mound to thunderous applause from the 55,820 fans cheering "U.S.A.! U.S.A.!" George W. Bush, the

President George W. Bush talks with Derek Jeter before throwing out the ceremonial first pitch in Game 3 of the 2001 World Series between the Diamondbacks and Yankees at Yankee Stadium. Jeter reportedly told the president, "Don't bounce it, they'll boo you." President Bush went out and threw a strike. (US National Archives, photograph by Eric Draper, via Wikimedia Commons)

forty-third President of the United States, waved to the New York crowd, and toed the Yankee Stadium pitcher's slab.

For the first time in forty-five years, a sitting president would throw out the ceremonial first pitch at a World Series game. Only four other presidents had ever thrown out the ceremonial first pitch at a World Series game while still serving in office, and none had made a Fall Classic pitch since Dwight Eisenhower did before the opening game of the 1956 Series at Ebbets Field in Brooklyn.

With little question, security at a World Series game has never been of more paramount concern than for President Bush's appearance at Yankee Stadium following the terrorist attacks. Though no one realized it at the time, there was an extra umpire on the field for the pre-game ceremony who turned out to be a Secret Service agent working undercover.

As the President reared back into his throwing motion, stretching his sweatshirt emblazoned with "FDNY," a tribute to the New York City Fire Department, the outline of a bullet-proof vest became visible. Seemingly unencumbered, the President fired a strike to the Yankees back-up catcher, Todd Greene. Suddenly, a convoy of Air Force military jets flying in a V-formation screamed over the stadium light stanchions.

Then the other marquee Texan, Roger Clemens, took the mound for the Yankees and overpowered the Diamondbacks with his fastball and sinker. The Rocket came up huge in a gut-check game, giving up only three singles and striking out nine Arizona batters in seven innings. Mariano Rivera got the final six outs with four strikeouts to nail down a crucial 2-1 victory, setting the stage for the unbelievable endings to Games 4 and 5.

2003

Boone Blasts Boston

Aaron Boone played in 54 games as a Yankee, but will be remembered in New York forever. His eleventh inning home run capped a dramatic comeback win over the archrival Boston Red Sox in Game 7 of the 2003 American League Championship Series, sending the giddy Yankees to their sixth World Series appearance in eight seasons.

Prior to hitting that legendary home run, Boone was famous for being a third-generation major league ballplayer. He is the son of former catcher Bob Boone (1972 to 1990), and the grandson of former infielder Ray Boone (1948 to 1960). His brother, Bret, also had a solid career as a major league infielder (1992 to 2005). The Boone family is the first family with three generations of All-Star players.

Aaron Boone came to New York from Cincinnati at the July 31st trading deadline to play third base. He hit .254 with six homers and 31 runs batted in for the Yankees. His bat was slumping at season's end, and his offensive frustrations continued into the postseason. In the first six games of the series against Boston, Boone was just two for 16, an anemic .125 batting average. Both hits were groundball dribblers that never left the infield. Manager Joe Torre benched Boone in the series-deciding seventh game in favor of Enrique Wilson, who hit .216 in four seasons with the Yankees.

In the seventh game, the Red Sox came out swinging against New York starting pitcher Roger Clemens, knocking out Clemens in the fourth inning already leading 4-0 and with two men on base and nobody out. The Red Sox seemed ready to turn the game into a blowout. Only three brilliant shutout innings by Mike Mussina (making the first relief appearance of his career after 400 starts) kept the Red Sox at bay. Boone sat on the bench watching for six innings. The Yankees trailed, 4-1, and had managed just three hits against Boston's masterful pitcher Pedro Martinez.

Finally, in the seventh inning the Yankees flexed a little muscle. Jason Giambi hit his second solo home run of the game to close the deficit to 4-2. In the top of the eighth,

David Ortiz homered to give the Red Sox a three-run cushion once again. The Yankees were six outs away from losing the pennant. Martinez had given Boston seven strong innings of work, and though the Boston bullpen was lights out all series, manager Grady Little decided to stick with his ace and sent Martinez back out to the mound to pitch the bottom the eighth inning.

The eighth inning started innocently enough, with Martinez retiring the first batter to face him. With one out and nobody on base, Derek Jeter doubled and Bernie Williams singled him home, prompting Little to walk to the mound to consult with his pitcher. Now, it seemed clear to all, Little would replaced his tiring ace with a fresh arm. Martinez must have assured his manager he still had something left in the tank, because Little had confidence in his three-time Cy Young Award-winning pitcher. Little allowed Martinez to stay in the game to face Hideki Matsui, a controversial move that will be forever debated among baseball fans. Matsui ripped a double down the right-field line and Jorge Posada followed with a two-run double to tie the game 5-5. Little signaled to the bullpen to replace Martinez.

The contest was far from over as both bullpens went in lockdown mode. Mariano Rivera came on for the Yankees in the ninth and pitched three shutout innings. Boston's Mike Timlin pitched a scoreless ninth and Tim Wakefield pitched a scoreless tenth. As the game moved into the bottom of the eleventh inning, Boone, who had entered earlier as a pinch-runner, was set to lead-off against Wakefield, a knuckleballer who had already won two games in the series.

"All I wanted," Boone would say later, "was to get on base, to make contact."

In one of the most dramatic scenes in baseball history, Boone launched Wakefield's first pitch into the left field seats for a pennant-winning home run, propelling the Yankees into the World Series, and once again breaking the hearts of Red Sox Nation. As Boone jumped on home plate with both feet, Rivera, the series most valuable player, raced to the pitcher's mound and collapsed atop the rubber, part joyous celebration, part exhaustion, before being carried off the field on his teammates' shoulders.

"You always emulate these moments in your backyard," Boone would say. "I still can't put the feeling into words . . . I'm floating."

The Yankees moved quickly to re-sign Boone after the season. Unfortunately for him, his hero status among New Yorkers was abruptly cut short when he tore a left knee ligament during a pick-up basketball game the following January. The injury voided Boone's contractand New York quickly replaced him by trading for the Texas Rangers' Alex Rodriguez.

Aaron Boone celebrates his walk-off, pennant-winning home run in the bottom of the eleventh inning against the Red Sox in the 2003 ALCS. (AP Photo/Bill Kostroun, File)

2005

A-Rod's Big Night

Alex Rodriguez proved to be a one-man wrecking crew when the Yankees demolished the Los Angeles Angels of Anaheim in a 12-4 rout at Yankee Stadium, on April 26, 2005. Rodriguez hit three home runs in his first three at-bats and became only the eleventh major league player with ten or more runs batted in in a game. It was surely his greatest game in pinstripes.

All three blasts were hit off Bartolo Colon, who would win the Cy Young Award that season. Alex's first home run was a three-run moon shot high over the left-centerfield wall. His second homer was a two-run blast lined into the same area. His third homer, a grand slam, was a towering drive that crashed into the centerfield bleachers some 475 feet away. In his first three at-bats, Rodriguez had three home runs and nine runs batted in—but he wasn't done. He added a run-scoring single in the sixth inning and finished with 10 runs batted in, falling one short of the American League record of 11, set by the Yankees' Tony Lazzeri in 1936. St. Louis Cardinal players Jim Bottomley (1924) and Mark Whiten (1993) share the major league single-game record of 12 RBIs.

"When I got to first base after that last hit, I was on top of a cloud," said Rodriguez. "You definitely don't want a moment like that to end. Tonight was one of those magical nights. You want it to last forever. This is definitely a night I'll never forget."

Later that year, he slugged his 400th career home run on June 8, 2005—making him the youngest ever to reach that mark. Rodriguez was twenty-nine years and 316 days old; Ken Griffey, Jr., the previous record holder, reached 400 home runs at thirty years, 141 days. Rodriguez also is the youngest ever to hit 500 and 600 homers. He hit his 500th career home run against Kansas City Royals pitcher Kyle Davies at Yankee Stadium, on August 4, 2007, just eight days after his thirty-second birthday. On the three-year anniversary of hitting his 500th home run, he hit No. 600, at Yankee Stadium against Shaun Marcum of the Toronto Blue Jays. Fittingly, the ball landed on the netting atop Monument

171

Alex Rodriquez hit three home runs and had 10 RBI
against the Angels on April 26, 2005. (Keith Allison
via Wikimedia Commons)

Park in center field. At thirty-five years and eight days old, he was again the youngest to
reach the milestone. At the time, many observers picked him as the slugger most likely to
be the next challenger to baseball's career home run mark held by Barry Bonds with 762.

Rodriguez was without question one of the greatest players ever to play the game. He
was a complete player. He could run, throw, field, and hit with the best. His powerful bat
produced eye-popping statistics. During his eighteen full seasons in the major leagues, he
batted .300 or better nine times, hit 30 or more home runs 15 times, won five home run
titles, and three Most Valuable Player awards.

Rodriguez had surgery to repair a torn labrum in his right hip prior to the 2009 season. He returned to the team on May 8 in Baltimore at Camden Yards and hit a three-run
home run on the first pitch he saw from Orioles starter Jeremy Guthrie in the Yankees' 4-0
victory. The team struggled early in the season without Rodriguez, but after his return, the
Yankees caught fire, winning the division and posting the best record in baseball.

On the final day of the 2009 season against the Tampa Bay Rays at Tropicana Field,
Alex hit a grand slam and a three-run home run in the sixth inning, becoming the first

American League player ever to drive in seven runs in an inning. (The major league record is eight and was set by Fernando Tatis of the St. Louis Cardinals, who hit two grand slams in an inning, on April 23, 1999.) With those blasts Rodriguez also set a major league record, becoming the first player to have thirteen seasons with at least 30 home runs and 100 runs batted in.

"It's magical," said Yankees hitting coach Kevin Long. "He comes in his first game in Baltimore and hits a home run, and then this last game he hits a grand slam. You just shake your head at the things he's able to do."

Among his 696 career home runs, Rodriguez hit a record 25 grand slams. He set a major league mark with his 24th career slam, passing Lou Gehrig's 75-year old record of 23 with a blast during a 5-1 Yankees victory over the San Francisco Giants on September 20, 2013. The shot came off a 2-1 pitch from George Kontos and flew over the right field fence to break a 1-1 tie.

Rodriguez had tied Gehrig with 23 career grand slams on June 12, 2012, in Atlanta. At the time, he spoke of his admiration for the former Yankees star. Gehrig's last grand slam came on August 20, 1938, when he was in his last full season with the Yankees. "I'm a huge fan of Lou Gehrig, everything he's done, going back to his college days in New York," Rodriguez said. "He's kind of the gold standard for a Yankee. It's a special moment. I'll think about it someday."

A-Rod extended his record to 25 "grand salamis" in a game between the Yankees and the Minnesota Twins. Trailing 4-1 with the bases loaded in the seventh inning, Rodriguez stepped up to the plate and launched a J.R. Graham 95-mile-per-hour fastball 420 feet away from home plate into the Yankees bullpen to give the Yankees a 5-4 lead. The go-ahead blast helped lift the Yankees to an 8-4 victory over the Twins. After his grand slam, the crowd of 38,007 summoned Rodriguez from the Yankees' dugout for a curtain call.

But despite his formidable gifts, Alex has never won the deep or lasting affection of fans, likely because of his huge contract, good looks, admitted use of performance enhancing drugs (after denying he used them), and a reputation for struggling in the postseason. That changed when Rodriguez shined during the 2009 playoffs. He hit a game-tying home run off Minnesota's Joe Nathan in the bottom of the ninth of Game 2 of the AL division series and in the championship series against the Angels, he hit .429 with three homers and six RBI. During a torrid seven-game stretch he hit five homers, drove in 11 runs and scored nine times. Rodriguez then won his first World Series when the Yankees defeated the Philadelphia Phillies in six games. A-Rod got a clutch hit in Game 4, driving in the go-ahead run with two outs in the ninth inning off closer Brad Lidge.

"It's wonderful to see," Reggie Jackson said of Rodriguez's postseason success. "I'm diggin' it. It's like watching a star in a movie. We all knew he had it in him. And when you see it come out like this, there's a real joy in it."

THE BIG SWITCH

Following the 2003 season, the Texas Rangers traded Alex Rodriguez to the New York Yankees. The best player in baseball was bringing his skills to the most famous stage in all of sports: Yankee Stadium.

Before he became the Yankees' third baseman, Rodriguez was by far and away the most productive shortstop ever. Even though he had won two Gold Gloves as the Texas shortstop, Alex agreed to switch positions and become a third baseman when he joined the Yankees so Derek Jeter could remain at short. Alex was the best shortstop in the majors, but he knew the Yankees would be a better team with him and Jeter playing together. So like his hero, the Baltimore Orioles star Cal Ripken, Jr., he moved to third. But Ripken moved to third when he had gotten older and slower. Rodriguez was still in the prime of his career. His position switch was the selfless act of a team player.

Besides switching positions, Alex also had to switch uniform numbers. He had worn No. 3 his entire career as a tribute to another one of his idols; the former Atlanta Braves star Dale Murphy. But No. 3 is retired by the Yankees in honor of Babe Ruth, so Rodriguez decided to wear No. 13. It proved to be lucky for the new Yankees third baseman, for Rodriguez finished the 2005 season with a league-leading 48 homers. He won the AL Most Valuable Player award for the second time in three seasons, and became the only player to win the award for two different teams at two different positions.

In 2007, A-Rod hit 54 homers and won his third most valuable player award. His mark of 54 homers is the most homers ever hit in a season by a third baseman. Rodriguez now holds the records for most home runs in a single season at two positions, shortstop and third base.

Rodriquez was suspended for the entire 2014 season, the largest penalty for performance-enhancing drug use in baseball history. He returned as a DH in 2015 and hit 33 home runs and 86 RBI, an unexpectedly strong performance for a thirty-nine-year-old after a full-season layoff. After struggling for much of the 2016 season, A-Rod was unconditionally released in August to end his twelve seasons in pinstripes.

2008

From Catcher to Manager

The acquisition of Joe Girardi for the 1996 season was not a popular move with Yankees fans. He was replacing catcher Mike Stanley, who was an All-Star on the 1995 wild card team that reached the postseason for the first time since losing in the 1981 World Series. Stanley hit .305 with 26 home runs and 84 RBI in 1993, and he combined for 35 homers and 140 RBI during the 1994 and '95 seasons.

Joe Girardi has been involved in a number of miracle moments as both a Yankee player and manager. (Keith Allison via Wikimedia Commons)

"I remember walking into spring training, the first day, and people saying, 'Boy, you've got big shoes to fill,'" Girardi recalled. "I thought, well, I wear a size 13."

Girardi had a tough start in New York. Three weeks into his career as a Yankee, Girardi—a career .269 hitter with 18 home runs—was batting just .228 with 2 RBI. Fans missed Stanley, whom Girardi had replaced, and who was a better hitter. Girardi got booed mercilessly. The radio station WFAN mocked Girardi by playing a retooled version of the 1941 hit song "Joltin' Joe DiMaggio," in which the hosts would shout out "Girardio!" in place of "DiMaggio."

The cool welcome just made Girardi work harder, approaching the challenges methodically. "A fear of failure is what really drove me," he said, "and the only way I could not fail was to intellectually and physically prepare. So then whatever happened happened. I didn't want to ever face the unexpected."

Girardi said that Yankees fans stopped booing him after he caught Dwight Gooden's no-hitter at the Stadium, on May 14, 1996. He also started hitting better. Understanding that he wasn't the power hitter Stanley was, Girardi settled into his new surroundings and batted .304 after May 1. For the season he batted .294 and did a lot of little things to help the Yankees offensively. Girardi led the team with 11 sacrifice bunts, and his 13 stolen bases were third best. But as the Yankees rolled through the postseason, and moved to within a game of clinching the world championship, Girardi had yet to make a significant offensive contribution. He had only five hits in 28 postseason at-bats and had not driven in a single run.

That changed dramatically in Game 6 of the 1996 World Series. The Yankees had lost the first two games at home against the Braves, but then roared back to take the next three in Atlanta. Fans arrived in the Bronx stoked to celebrate what they hoped would be the Yankees' first World Series title since 1978. The Yankees struck against Atlanta pitcher Greg Maddux in the bottom of the third inning. Paul O'Neill led off the inning with a double and advanced to third on a groundout. Then Girardi sent a shot over the head of centerfielder Marquis Grissom. The ball landed on the warning track and bounced against the fence.

"I hit it and I thought I got a sac fly," Girardi said. "And then I saw it go over his head. I was just running as fast as I could."

As Girardi raced around the bases, O'Neill easily jogged home from third to give the Yankees a 1-0 lead. The fans in Yankee Stadium erupted.

"When I stepped on home plate, when I scored, I could actually feel the ground shaking," said O'Neill.

Girardi wasn't on third base for long. He scored on Derek Jeter's RBI single to make it 2-0, and the old Stadium got even louder. Television analyst Tim McCarver said to his broadcast partners Joe Buck and Bob Brenly, "Guys, our booth is shaking."

To which Brenly replied, "I think the whole city is shaking."

Bernie Williams then singled home Jeter and the Yankees led 3-0. Those were the only runs Maddux gave up in the series, but they were costly. The Yankees held on for a 3-2 victory and then popped the Champagne corks to celebrate the franchise's 23rd world title.

Of the 1,100 hits Girardi compiled during his 15-year playing career, the triple stands out as the most memorable, even if the actual moment is a bit fuzzy.

"It's a blur," Girardi said. "I wish I could have soaked it in more because it happened so fast. I hear Paul O'Neill talk about how the stands were shaking. I don't remember any of that. That's the one moment of time in my career I wish I could go back to."

Girardi's playing career with the Yankees lasted from 1996 to 1999, and during that time there was little disappointment, as the team won the World Series each year except 1997. Girardi was behind the plate to catch David Cone's perfect game at the Stadium, on Yogi Berra Day, July 18, 1999. After the final out, Cone dropped to his knees, and was swarmed by Girardi, who joined the pitcher in a massive bear hug. Then Girardi pulled Cone down on top of him.

"I didn't want to let go," said Cone. "That's how good I felt about Joe Girardi and what he means to me not only professionally but personally."

At the end of that year, Girardi became a free agent and signed with the Cubs, his original team. He was a solid defensive catcher with a positive reputation for being like another coach on the field. Ron Hassey, a former major league catcher who had been the Colorado Rockies' third-base coach when Girardi played there, said, "Joe understands that the most important job for a catcher is to get the most out of your pitcher. That includes pitch selection, blocking balls, throwing runners out, holding runners on, knowing the strengths and weaknesses of hitters. Joe's as good as there is at those things."

In all, he played for four teams during his career: with the Chicago Cubs (1989-92), the Colorado Rockies (1993-95), the New York Yankees (1996-99), the Cubs again (2000-2002), and, finally, as a 38-year-old backup catcher with the St. Louis Cardinals, playing his last game at Busch Stadium on September 20, 2003. The following year, he became a television commentator for the Yankees' YES network, but missed being in uniform. In 2005, he joined the team as the bench coach under manager Joe Torre. A year later, at 41, Girardi was hired to manage a National League franchise, the Florida Marlins.

Although the Marlins' annual payroll of about $15 million was the lowest in major league baseball, Girardi led the team into playoff contention until the end of the season, when the Marlins fell to fourth place. Still, in recognition for guiding a youthful team of overachievers, the baseball writers' association honored Girardi with the 2006 National League Manager of the Year award. This success, however, did not help him keep his job. Jeffrey Loria, the Marlins' owner, fired Girardi in October. According to reports, Girardi was done for after he told Loria to calm down during a game when Loria was yelling at an umpire from the stands. Whatever the reason, Girardi, perhaps aware he would have opportunities elsewhere, didn't seem all that upset about being let go.

"It was short, brief, and unemotional," he said about his time in Florida.

Girardi returned to the Yankees' broadcast booth for the 2007 season, Joe Torre's last as manager. New York made the playoffs in all 12 years under Torre, who won the World Series in four of his first five seasons. Finding a manager to replace Torre would not be easy.

When the Yankees needed a big hit to propel them to victory in the clinching game of Torre's first World Series, it was Girardi who got it. A triple to center field off Greg Maddux sparked the Yankees to the 1996 title that started their dynasty. Eleven years later, with Torre gone, the Yankees needed Girardi again, this time as the manager to steer them back to the World Series.

Yankees general manager Brian Cashman was impressed by three attributes he saw in Girardi: hard work, accountability and discipline. "He likes to compete all the time," Cashman said. "We believe he's mentally tough."

The team and Girardi agreed to a three-year contract and a mandate to deliver World Series championship No. 27.

"I expect to be playing in the fall classic next October. I think that's everyone's expectation," Girardi said.

Girardi needed to be mentally tough. Just as he had a tough time following Mike Stanley when he joined the Yankees as a player, he now found himself replacing a beloved manager.

"I can't be Joe Torre because I'm made up different," Girardi said. "I'm a different character, so I don't worry about how I'm going to replace someone. I'm more worried about just being myself and getting the most out of the guys."

But Girardi also was well aware of the lofty expectations he would face and what's demanded of a Yankees manager, especially following in Torre's footsteps. Torre, after all, made the playoffs in each of his 12 seasons in the Bronx but was let go after going seven years without a World Series championship. So Girardi put the bull's-eye on his back, taking uniform No. 27 in recognition of the fact the Yankees were chasing their 27th title.

The press began by portraying Girardi as controlling and demanding, a robotic technocrat. His first spring training as the Yankees' manager was likened to boot camp. One day, both the *Post* and the *News* ran photographs of Girardi, with his signature crewcut, under the words "G.I. Joe." The Yankees broke a string of 13 straight postseason appearances in 2008, Girardi's first year in the Bronx, but hard work prevailed. Two years later, he redeemed himself with a 2009 team that won 103 games and cruised to a World Series title with an 11-4 playoff record. Following the team's 2009 World Series triumph over the Phillies, Girardi changed his number to 28, signifying a new goal. He guided the

Yankees to postseason appearances in 2010, 2011, and 2012, averaging nearly 96 wins per season, and also claimed an AL wild card in 2015.

Now the Yankees are a team in transition. Gone are the veteran superstars like Derek Jeter, Mariano Rivera, Alex Rodriguez, and Mark Teixeira. They are replaced on the roster by a group of young prospects with untapped potential, including Gary Sanchez, who made a strong case for Rookie of the Year honors after his major league call-up in August of 2016. No matter what happens, though, Girardi is confident the franchise is headed down the right track with its current youth movement.

"It has been a big turnover, and that happens in this game, but I think we've seen some huge improvements and good things all around, and I think there's some answers here," Girardi said. "I've been here a long time and seen some of these older guys do a lot of great things, but I believe our kids are going to do great things and win some championships, too."

By pushing the right buttons, and having a little luck, Girardi might soon be wearing jersey No. 29. Stay tuned.

2008

The Captain Closes the Stadium

The Yankees played in the original Yankee Stadium from 1923 to 1973. After completing the Stadium's fiftieth anniversary season, a complete remodeling began. The 1974 and 1975 Yankees played in Shea Stadium for two years while Yankee Stadium was torn down and rebuilt. The remodeled Yankee Stadium was christened on April 15, 1976, with an 11-4 rout of the Minnesota Twins. Just as they had in 1923, the Yankees opened their new stadium in grand style by reaching the World Series, though it would be another year before they captured the championship trophy. In all, the Yankees won 10 American League pennants and six World Series titles in the remodeled Yankee Stadium (1977, 1978, 1996, 1998, 1999, and 2000).

In 2006, a groundbreaking ceremony was held for a new Yankee Stadium to be ready for the 2009 season. The remodeled original Yankee Stadium took its final bow during the 2008 season, hosting that year's All-Star Game, won by the American League 4-3 in 15 innings. The building hosted its final home game on September 21. Gates opened early to allow fans to visit Monument Park and walk around the ballpark. With a national television audience watching, the Yankees starters took their positions in the field alongside all-time Yankee greats. Babe Ruth's daughter, Julia Ruth Stevens, threw out the ceremonial first pitch.

In the bottom of the seventh inning, longtime public address announcer Bob Sheppard appeared on the scoreboard's video screen. He recited a poem he had written just for the occasion. "Farewell, old Yankee Stadium, farewell. What a wonderful story you can tell. DiMaggio, Mantle, Gehrig and Ruth, a baseball cathedral in truth."

Fittingly, the Yankees won the game 7-3 over the Baltimore Orioles. Andy Pettitte got the win, Jose Molina hit the last home run and Mariano Rivera recorded the final three outs. After the final out, the players gathered near the pitcher's mound as captain Derek Jeter took the microphone and thanked the fans for their years of support, while reminding everyone of the new memories soon to be made.

Out with the old . . . Yankee Stadium in 2008 (Wikimedia Commons)

In with the new . . .Yankee Stadium in 2014. (Wikimedia Commons)

"From all of us up here, it's a huge honor to put this uniform on every day and come out here and play," said Jeter. "Every member of this organization, past and present, has been calling this place home for eighty-five years. There's a lot of tradition, a lot of history and a lot of memories. The great thing about memories is you're able to pass them along from generation to generation. Although things are going to change next year and we're going to move across the street, there are a few things with the New York Yankees that never change. That's pride, tradition, and most of all we have the greatest fans in the world. We're relying on you to take the memories from this stadium and add them to the new memories we make at the new Yankee Stadium and continue to pass them on from generation to generation. We just want to take this moment to salute you, the greatest fans in the world."

Then the players walked around the warning track, waving to fans, and saying good-bye to the stadium.

MONUMENT PARK

Monument Park is an open-air Yankee Stadium museum located behind the center field fence. It is a collection of monuments, plaques, and retired numbers that honor former Yankees greats. On game days, it is a tourist attraction for fans of all ages that wish to immerse themselves in the franchise's storied history. There are six monuments in Monument Park honoring individuals and one for the victims and heroes of September 11, 2001. In all, there are also 24 plaques: 16 for Yankees players and managers, two for Yankees executives, two for Yankee Stadium personnel, three for papal visits, and one for the Yankees insignia.

The first monument was dedicated in 1932 for manager Miller Huggins, who died unexpectedly during the 1929 season. The first plaque was placed on the center field wall in 1940 in tribute to former owner Jacob Ruppert. The Yankees dedicated a monument to Babe Ruth on April 19, 1949, eight months after his death. The inscription is memorably brief for such an outsize man; three lines of gold-faced letters read: "A Great Ball Player/A Great Man/A Great American." The 4,700-pound monument joined the tributes to Huggins and Lou Gehrig already located within the field of play. Fans could see the large stone monuments, giving some youngsters the impression that the remains of the Yankee greats were buried under their tombstones.

In the original Yankee Stadium, the monuments were in fair territory and part of the playing field. The monuments and a flagpole were located in straightaway center field on the warning track approximately 10 feet in front of the wall. Sometimes long hits and fly balls forced fielders to go behind the monuments to retrieve the baseball.

Every Yankees fan knows the significance of those hallowed stones in Monument Park. The greatest names of this most storied franchise are represented. Those honored have claimed it is a distinction more precious than even a Hall of Fame induction.

Babe Ruth's monument in the old Yankee Stadium. (Wikimedia Commons)

2009

Godzilla Conquers Gotham

A new era in the history of the New York Yankees began on April 16, 2009 when the team played its first game at the new Yankee Stadium against the Cleveland Indians. The ghosts of the old Yankee Stadium seemed to have moved across the street to the new stadium, because by season's end the Yankees would win their 27th world championship.

With offseason additions C.C. Sabathia, Mark Teixeira and A.J. Burnett proving to be difference-makers, the Yankees won a major league best 103 games in 2009 and then powered through the postseason. After sweeping the Minnesota Twins in three games to win the divisional series, and then winning their 40th American League pennant by defeating the Los Angeles Angels of Anaheim in six games, the Yankees advanced to the World Series

Along with A.J. Burnett, C.C. Sabathia and Mark Teixeria proved to key to the Yankees' winning a championship in 2009. (Keith Allison via Wikimedia Commons)

for the first time since 2003. That year was Japanese home run champion Hideki Matsui's first season with the Yankees, which ended with a World Series loss to the Florida Marlins.

Six years later, the Yankees were back on baseball's biggest stage, where they would face the defending champion Philadelphia Phillies in the 2009 World Series. Since Matsui was the designated hitter, he didn't start any of the games played in Philadelphia, but that didn't lessen his impact. "Godzilla" had a huge Series, going 8 for 13 for a .615 batting average with three home runs and eight runs batted in.

"My first and foremost goal when I joined the Yankees was to win the world championship," Matsui said through his interpreter. "Certainly, it's been a long road and very difficult journey. But I'm just happy that after all these years we were able to win and reach the goal that I had come here for."

Hideki Matsui was the 2009 World Series MVP. (Keith Allison via Wikimedia Commons)

In the series-clinching sixth game, Matsui almost single-handedly defeated the Phillies. He hit a two-run home run in the second inning, a two-run single in the third and a two-run double in the fifth, helping lead the Yankees to a 7-3 victory. Matsui drove in six runs, tying the single-game World Series record, and he was the obvious choice for World Series most valuable player, the first full-time designated hitter (and Japanese player) to earn the award. Bobby Richardson was the only other player with six RBIs in a World Series game, doing it for the Yankees in Game 3 against the Pittsburgh Pirates in 1960. Richardson hit a first-inning grand slam and a two-run single in the fourth.

"I guess you could say this is the best moment of my life right now," Matsui said.

"They're partying in Tokyo tonight," said teammate Nick Swisher.

Matsui finished the series with six hits in his final nine at-bats, including three home runs. Nothing, though, topped his Game 6 performance, when Matsui's history-making offensive output resulted in his raising of a championship trophy.

"He looked like he wanted it bad," Derek Jeter said. "Matsui is one of my favorite players. He's one of my favorite teammates. He comes ready to play every day. He's a professional hitter. All he wants to do is win."

"It's awesome," Matsui said. "Unbelievable. I'm surprised myself."

Veteran left-hander Andy Pettitte, pitching on three days' rest, threw five and two-thirds solid innings, allowing three runs on four hits. He earned his fifth World Series ring with his second victory of the series. Pettitte's 2009 postseason was one for the ages: he became the first pitcher in baseball history to start and win the clinching games in the division series, championship series and World Series in the same postseason. (He also won the regular season game that clinched the American League East.)

On his way to five World Series championships, Andy won 19 postseason games, more than any other pitcher in baseball history. He's also the all-time postseason leader in games started (44) and innings pitched (276.2). With a career record of 256-153, he is one of 13 pitchers since 1900 with at least 200 wins, a career winning percentage of .600 and a record more than 100 games above .500. Remarkably, he never had a losing season. As far as where he falls in Yankees history, he's the franchise's all-time leader in strikeouts (2,020), ranks first in games started (438, tied with Whitey Ford), and is third in wins (219, behind Ford and Red Ruffing).

Pettitte was an intense pitcher, standing on the mound, glaring at opposing batters, cap pulled tightly down on his forehead, glove held up to shield his face from the batter, so only his piercing eyes were visible as he looked in for a sign from the catcher.

"He had that ability to always dial it up when we needed him," said Yankees manager Joe Girardi, an ex-catcher who was a teammate and manager to Pettitte. "That's a guy that you want on the mound in pivotal games."

Andy Pettitte is the all-time postseason leader in games started, innings pitched, and wins. (Chris Ptacek via Wikimedia Commons)

YANKEES WORLD SERIES MOST VALUABLE PLAYERS*

Year	Player	Position	Opponent
1956	Don Larsen	Pitcher	Brooklyn Dodgers
1958	Bob Turley	Pitcher	Milwaukee Braves
1960	Bobby Richardson	Second base	Pittsburgh Pirates
1961	Whitey Ford	Pitcher	Cincinnati Reds
1962	Ralph Terry	Pitcher	San Fran Giants
1977	Reggie Jackson	Outfield	LA Dodgers
1978	Bucky Dent	Shortstop	LA Dodgers
1996	John Wetteland	Pitcher	Atlanta Braves
1998	Scott Brosius	Third base	San Diego Padres
1999	Mariano Rivera	Pitcher	Atlanta Braves
2000	Derek Jeter	Shortstop	New York Mets
2009	Hideki Matsui	Designated hitter	Philadelphia Phillies

*First awarded in 1955

2011

Mo Is Money

A flicker of anticipation ran through the grandstand as an excited crowd of 43,201 people inched forward in their seats. The Yankees were holding on to a four run lead against the Toronto Blue Jays at Yankee Stadium, on May 25, 2011. The game moved to the top of the ninth inning with the home team just three outs away from a victory—the three toughest outs in baseball to record. Now entering the game was Mariano Rivera, a reedy right-handed relief pitcher from Panama with a steely focus and a sense of mental calm so great he could sleep through a thunderstorm.

If there is one relief pitcher in the last decade that might personify the word "closer," a stadium full of baseball experts might pick Rivera. Few, if any, relief pitchers enjoy the immensely positive reputation for finality that Rivera has earned with the Yankees. As team captain Derek Jeter says: "When he comes in the game, the mindset is, it's over."

The game against the Blue Jays was a typical appearance. The forty-one-year-old reliever faced four batters, got three outs, threw just 12 pitches, 10 for strikes. But it was not a typical appearance, it was special, for Rivera became the first pitcher in major league baseball history to have appeared in 1,000 games for one team (and the fifteenth to reach the plateau overall).

"It's a blessing to be able to be on the same team and do that. It's not too often you see that. But the most important thing is that we won," Rivera said after retiring the side in the ninth inning of the Yankees' 7-3 win over Toronto.

The vision of Rivera bursting through the bullpen door is enough to give even the most malevolent opposing hitters serious pause. With the Yankee Stadium sound system blaring Metallica's "Enter Sandman," and the fans raucously cheering in anticipation, he jogs across the outfield grass, strides gracefully to the mound, fires seven or eight warm-up pitches, stares blankly at his target with shark-like eyes, and then gets down to serious business.

"The song starts playing, the game's over," says former teammate Jason Giambi.

Despite the perilous situation and the swelling crowd noise, whether for him or against him, any time Rivera arrives for his rescue act, he resists the pressure simply by ignoring it. Occasionally he isn't even aware of the identity of the man swinging the bat at home plate. In former manager Joe Torre's opinion, he has the ideal temperament for a closer.

"He's the best I've ever been around. Not only the ability to pitch and perform under pressure, but the calm he puts over the clubhouse."

Rivera doesn't quarrel with that view.

"I don't get nervous. I trust God. If I get nervous, I can't do my job."

More than anyone else, it was Rivera doing his job that propelled the Yankees into World Series champions five times, as he was on the mound to record the final out in four clinching games in 1998, 1999, 2000, and 2009. October after October, the 6-foot-2, 185-pounder held precarious leads the Yankees had scratched together. He literally attacked rival hitters with one pitch: an unsolvable cut fastball that has been called a combination of thunder and location.

Rivera's impact couldn't possibly be any greater. His lifetime postseason earned run average of 0.70 is the major league record. During the Yankees' memorable 1998 season, Rivera did not give up a run in the postseason. He did the same again in 1999, when he was the World Series most valuable player. More impressive still, his record 42 postseason saves, including 11 in the World Series, are 24 more than his next closest competitor, Brad Lidge (18), which explains why Rivera's teammates act as if they are about to inherit the family trust fund.

"Our whole game plan [was] to get a lead and give the ball to him in the ninth inning," said Paul O'Neill, an ex-teammate.

Rivera became the king of all closers after passing Trevor Hoffman with his record-setting 602nd save by pitching a perfect ninth inning in a 6-4 win over the Minnesota Twins at Yankee Stadium, on September 19, 2011. After he had been mobbed by his teammates, his longtime catcher Jorge Posada pushed Rivera back out to the mound so the crowd could salute him one more time. Asked to describe that moment, Rivera said: "Oh, my God. For the first time in my career, I'm on the mound alone. There's no one behind me, no one in front of me. I can't describe that feeling because it was priceless."

Final inventory figures for his career will show that all other relief pitchers will be shooting at his mark of 652 saves for a long time to come. But Mariano Rivera's contributions go beyond mere numbers, impressive as the numbers happen to be. It's the form as well as the substance that makes Rivera a star in the grand old Yankee tradition: humble, gracious, poised, and commanding. That he's also a spiritual and faithful man makes him all the more valuable as an inspiration to his teammates and his opponents.

"On the field and off the field, he's a Hall of Famer," said opposing manager Ozzie Guillen. "Young people should look up to him. He's the perfect player. God bless Mariano."

To Yankee fans, Guillen is preaching to the choir.

2011

Mr. 3,000

With one out in the third inning it was Derek Jeter's turn at bat in a game against the Tampa Bay Rays at Yankee Stadium, on Saturday, July 9, 2011. Not a single person visited the concession stand or the bathroom. Every spectator was in the ballpark, off their seat, standing on toes, craning necks, for what they hoped would be the best view of history.

Jeter had come into the game needing two hits for 3,000 in his charmed career, which would make him the twenty-eighth major league player, and the first as a Yankee, to record 3,000 hits. Flame throwing left-handed pitcher David Price was on the mound for Tampa. In his first at-bat Jeter worked the count to 3-2 and Price threw a 95-mile-per-hour fastball that Jeter smacked to left field for hit No. 2,999. The crowd roared its approval. They wanted to witness history.

Two innings later, Jeter connected on a full-count curveball, swinging his shiny black bat and sending the ball into the left-field bleachers to reach the 3,000-hit mark in the most thrilling way possible—by hitting a home run. It was magical that on his second hit of the day, in his second at-bat, Jeter—No. 2—reached his historic milestone at 2:00 p.m. It was Jeter's first homer at Yankee Stadium in nearly a year.

His teammates jumped joyously over the dugout railing and poured onto the field. Even the relievers ran in from the bullpen. All of them were waiting to celebrate at home plate as their captain rounded the bases. Raising a fist quickly in the air, Jeter ran head down, suppressing the urge to smile. Jorge Posada was the first to greet Jeter at home plate. Posada is Jeter's best friend on the Yankees, a teammate since 1992, when they were playing Class A ball in Greensboro, North Carolina. The two friends met in an overpowering embrace.

"I told him I was proud of him," said Posada.

Mariano Rivera, the third remaining Yankee from the dynasty teams of the 1990s, was right behind Posada, as was a receiving line of welcoming teammates. The applause and acclaim from the Yankee Stadium crowd of 48,103 lasted about four minutes. Jeter

191

Derek Jeter watches his home run for his 3,000th career hit during the third inning of a game against the Tampa Bay Rays on Saturday, July 9, 2011, at Yankee Stadium. (AP Photo/Bill Kostroun)

responded to the rousing ovation with a pair of curtain calls, turning to each corner of the stadium to accept the congratulations. Then Jeter tipped his batting helmet to his family in a private box high above the first-base line with his right hand.

"If I would have tried to have written it and given it to someone, I wouldn't have even bought it," said Jeter. "It's just one of those special days."

But Jeter was far from done. He doubled in the fifth inning, singled in the sixth and drove in the go-ahead run with another single in the eighth, matching a career high by going 5 for 5 as the Yankees beat the Rays, 5-4.

"The thing that means the most to me is that I've been able to get all these hits in a Yankee uniform," said Jeter. "No one's been able to do that before, which is hard to believe. I've grown up with these fans. They've seen me since I've been twenty years old."

Jeter recorded 2,914 hits from 1996 to 2010, the most in baseball in that span. He amassed more hits as a Yankee than Gehrig, Ruth, DiMaggio or Mantle. As was Gehrig before him, Jeter's name and reputation are similarly exalted in today's game, and the kid from Kalamazoo who loves his parents and respects the game is a sure first ballot Hall of Famer.

"It's unbelievable what he does," says manager Joe Girardi. "He's so consistent. He gets 200 hits a year, every year. They're normal Derek Jeter years, but all those normal years add up to greatness."

GRAND SLAM HISTORY

Two months after Derek Jeter reached 3,000 career hits, the Yankees set a remarkable team home run record. The Yankees became the first team in major league history to hit three grand slams in a game, with Robinson Cano, Russell Martin, and Curtis Granderson connecting in a 22-9 rout over the Oakland Athletics at Yankee Stadium, on August 25, 2011. Cano began the assault with a fifth-inning slam off A's starter Rich Harden. Then Martin connected in the sixth off Fautino De Los Santos. Granderson launched his slam in the eighth off Bruce Billings.

Along with Russell Martin and Curtis Granderson, second-baseman Robinson Cano hit a grand slam in a game against the A's on August 25, 2011. (Keith Allison via Wikimedia Commons)

2016

Baby Bombers

Prior to the 2016 trade deadline, the Yankees decided to be sellers for the first time in over twenty-five years. Pitchers Aroldis Chapman, Andrew Miller and Ivan Nova, and outfielder Carlos Beltran were all traded to other contending teams in return for highly touted prospects. (Chapman and Miller wound up helping their respective teams—the Cubs and Indians—get to the 2016 World Series.) As part of their sudden youth movement, the Yankees also released Alex Rodriguez, who had 696 career home runs—trailing only Babe Ruth (714), Hank Aaron (755) and Barry Bonds (762) on the all time list.

On the same day the Yankees honored their 1996 World Series championship team, a new era of Yankees baseball began with a bang. Tyler Austin and Aaron Judge, who were called up by the Yankees from Triple-A Scranton/Wilkes-Barre prior to a game against the Tampa Bay Rays, didn't wait long to prove they belonged in the major leagues. Austin and Judge made their debuts in stunning fashion during the Yankees' 8-4 win at Yankee Stadium on August 13, 2016. The teammates hammered back-to-back home runs in their first at-bats in the second inning to give New York a 2-0 lead. Austin and Judge became the first teammates to hit home runs in their first major league at-bats in the same game. They are also the first teammates to homer in their debuts in the same game and became the fourth and fifth players in Yankees history to hit home runs in their first career plate appearance, joining John Miller, Andy Phillips and Marcus Thames.

"You can't draw it up any better when you call up two young players," Yankees manager Joe Girardi said.

With two out in the second inning, Austin faced Rays right-hander Matt Andriese and with a 2-2 count drove a 92-mile-per-hour fastball just over the 314-foot sign near the foul pole in right field, which prompted Austin to pump his fist in celebration. "I don't think I could've asked for anything better," Austin said. "It's pretty awesome."

Then Judge followed and with a 1-2 count he connected with Andriese's 87-mile-per-hour changeup and drove a mammoth blast over the center field wall. The homer was a no-doubter the moment it left the bat. Judge's towering homer traveled 457 feet, making it the fourth-longest home run ever hit at the new Yankee Stadium, behind Raul Ibanez (477 feet), Alex Rodriguez (460 feet), Carlos Correa (459 feet) and Mark Trumbo (also 457 feet).

"It was exciting," Judge said. "Tyler went out there and he got down 0-2 really quick, but he battled and had a great at-bat and was able to hit one out. I was ecstatic on deck and I was like, 'I've just got to make contact now.' What a day. That's all I can really say."

With the homer, Judge became just the third player to hit the ball off or over the glass panels above Monument Park, joining Seattle's Russell Branyan in 2009 and Houston's Carlos Correa in 2016.

The next day, Judge swatted a solo shot in the Yankees' 12-3 loss to Tampa Bay. He became the second Yankee to homer in each of his first two major-league games. The first to accomplish this feat was Joe Lefebvre, who homered on May 22 and 23, 1980 (the latter as a pinch-hitter). Judge was only two games into his major-league career, but the twenty-four-year-old Californian with immense size (6'7", 275 pounds) had already nudged his way into the record books on consecutive days.

The promotion of Austin and Judge to the big league club reunited them with fellow prospect Gary Sanchez, the twenty-three-year-old catcher who had been their teammate at Scranton/Wilkes-Barre and who had beaten them to the Bronx, arriving in early August. And what a month of August it was for Sanchez. He was named the American League Player of the Week in consecutive weeks, and he became the first rookie in MLB history to accomplish that feat. He won the award the first time by batting .524 (11-for-21) with four home runs and six RBIs. He followed that with a nearly identical week, batting .522 (12-for-23) with five homers and nine RBIs, including a stretch in which he homered in three straight games. His 11 home runs in his first 23 games are also a feat never accomplished by anyone before.

"It feels great to win the award, but the reality is that the focus is to keep winning games right now," Sanchez said through a translator.

Aside from the honor of being named the player of the week, Sanchez received a watch from MLB in recognition of the award. Asked what he would do with two watches, Sanchez said, "I don't know. I haven't even gotten the first one yet." That proved that one month into his pro career, Major League Baseball could not keep up with Gary Sanchez's spectacular accomplishments.

By earning back-to-back AL Player of the Week honors, Sanchez was an easy choice for voters of the AL Player of the Month award. Sanchez hit .389 with 11 home runs, 21 RBI, nine doubles and 20 runs scored in 24 games during the month of August. Sanchez, who also

After being promoted to the Yankees in August as part of the team's 2016 youth movement, catcher Gary Sanchez went on an historic tear. (Keith Allison via Wikimedia Commons)

earned A.L. Rookie of the Month honors, is the first Yankees catcher ever to win either award. He's the first Yankee to win Player of the Month since Curtis Granderson in August 2011 and the first to win Rookie of the Month since Robinson Cano in September 2005.

"Pretty impressive considering what he's done," manager Joe Girardi said. "Coming up at an important time and facing good teams, it's really impressive."

Since the promotion of Sanchez from Triple-A on August 3, the Yankees began playing much better baseball and even climbed back into wild-card contention for a little while. "I think it's hard not to look at Gary Sanchez and be in awe of what he's done," said Girardi, who installed Sanchez as his everyday catcher and No. 3 hitter.

"It's been amazing what he's been able to do," said pitcher C.C. Sabathia. "He's brought energy to the team."

New York's faster-than-anticipated youth movement helped to keep the club's postseason hopes alive in 2016 and positioned the Yankees for even more success in 2017 and beyond.

REFERENCES

Books

Baseball: The Biographical Encyclopedia. David Pietrusza, Matthew Silverman and Michael Gershman. (New York: Total Sports Illustrated, 2000).

The Complete New York Yankees. Derek Gentile. (New York: Black Dog & Leventhal Publishers, 2001).

Diamonds: The Evolution of the Ballpark. Michael Gershman. (Boston: Houghton Mifflin Company, 1993).

Joe, You Coulda Made Us Proud. Joe Pepitone with Berry Stainback (New York: Sports Publishing, 2010).

New York Yankees Information & Record Guide. New York Yankees Official Publication. 2016.

One Hundred Years, New York Yankees, The Official Retrospective. (New York: Ballantine Books, 2003).

The Series: An Illustrated History of Baseball's Postseason Showcase. Joe Hoppel. (St. Louis: The Sporting News Publishing Company, 1990).

Yankees Century: 100 Years of New York Yankees Baseball. Glenn Stout. (Boston: Houghton Mifflin Company, 2002).

The Yankees: The Four Fabulous Eras of Baseball's Most Famous Team. Dave Anderson, Murray Chass, Robert Creamer and Harold Rosenthal. (New York: Random House, 1979).

Yankees World Series Memories. Maury Allen. (Champaign, Illinois: Sports Publishing L.L.C., 2008).

Periodicals and Websites

Associated Press

Baseball-Almanac.com

BaseballHallofFame.org

Baseball-Reference.com

ESPN.com

MLB.com

New York Times

NewYork.Yankees.MLB.com

The Sporting News

Sports Illustrated

USA Today

ACKNOWLEDGMENTS

This book would not have been possible without the creativity, sound judgment, and tireless work of my collaborators. The scope of the book was greatly enhanced by the imagination of Niels Aaboe, executive editor, Skyhorse Publishing. Many thanks to Niels and his colleagues, Kirsten Dalley, Tom Lau, and Spencer Samelson, for keeping me honest. Naturally, this project would have been difficult to complete without the understanding and support of my wife, Carolyn, and my children, Rachel and Jack.

Many others contributed ideas, time, advice and encouragement. They include John Flock, Seth Friedman, Michael Fischer, William Fischer, Carl Gedon, William Sokol, Matthew Kohut, David Griffel and Louis Griffel. To all of them, and to numerous other friends and associates who shared my vision, my deep and abiding thanks.